Eating Fresh from the Organic Garden State

A YEAR-ROUND GUIDE TO COOKING & BUYING LOCAL ORGANIC PRODUCTS

N·O·F·A

NEW·JERSEY

COMPILED & EDITED BY FRAN McMANUS
FOR THE NORTHEAST ORGANIC FARMING ASSOCIATION–NEW JERSEY
ILLUSTRATIONS BY ANNA SPRAGUE

Dedicated to small farms all over the world and to the courageous, hardworking farmers who run them

Eating Fresh from the Organic Garden State.

Published by NOFA-NJ
Copyright ©1997 by NOFA-NJ

Illustrations copyright ©1997 by Anna Sprague

Excerpt from *J. Howard Garrett's Organic Manual* by J. Howard Garrett reprinted with permission from the Summit Publishing Group, excerpt from *Nutrition Action Health Letter* reprinted with permission from the Center for Science in the Public Interest, Jersey Fresh Availability chart reprinted with permission from the New Jersey Department of Agriculture, Preservation and Storage chart by Julie Rawson reprinted with permission from NOFA-Massachusetts, excerpt from "Pesticides: What You Don't Know Can Hurt You" by Sharlene K. Johnson reprinted with permission from *Ladies' Home Journal*.

Cover design and illustrations: Anna Sprague
Book design: Fran McManus
Copy editor: Wendy Rickard Bollentin
Recipe editor: Martha Hester Stafford
Recipe tester: Joseph George
Proofreader: Paula Plantier

Printed in the United States of America on recycled paper.

First Edition

ISBN 1–883354–01–3
Library of Congress Catalog Card Number: 97–69420

acknowledgments

When I first conceived of this book, I envisioned something simple, with one chef and one author. It was Donna Batcho's energy and enthusiasm that made it possible to expand the scope of the project and to include so many talented chefs and contributing authors. I thank her for always pushing the limits of the book and for her tireless efforts to promote the idea that organic agriculture is good for the Garden State.

I want also to extend heartfelt thanks to the many people who donated their time and talents to this book: To the chefs who were inspiring both in the depth of their commitment to local organic produce and in their willingness to help make this book a reality. To Hilary Baum for keeping me on track by asking all the tough questions. To Jennifer Wilkins for providing a clear and positive view of how we can work together to keep small farms in our region viable. To Mindy Pennybacker of Mothers & Others for taking time to contribute to the book while on a deadline with her own. To Michele Bassler and Emily Brown Rosen of NOFA-NJ for enduring endless questions about the process and philosophy of organic farming. And to

Like many of the ideas presented in these pages, this guide was very much a local, organic effort. From the farmers to the chefs, to the many professionals and sponsors who contributed their time and energy, we reaffirmed what we always knew: that top-notch ingredients go a long way toward creating a superior product.

The main support for this project comes from the Geraldine R. Dodge Foundation, the New Jersey Department of Agriculture, and Kings Super Markets. The support given by those organizations is testimony to their commitment to the future of organic agriculture in New Jersey.

My special thanks to Alice Waters, who has long championed the culinary, environmental, and economic benefits of supporting local, organic produce. She may have left New Jersey, but her willingness to be a part of this project is evidence of her lasting affection for both our region and the best-tasting organic tomatoes anywhere. We are grateful to her for writing the wonderful foreword to this book.

I am especially grateful to Joan Gussow, whose writings and other works inspired me down this organic path; to Gary Hirshberg of Stonyfield Farm for the support he has so generously given to the cause of creating viable communities of local organic farms; to Art Brown, New Jersey Secretary of Agriculture, for his personal and professional interest in encouraging the growth of organic agriculture in New Jersey; and to the many chefs who contributed their time and artistic talents to the creation of this book. Working with these outstanding professionals has been an experience I will never forget.

Without the knowledge and expertise of Anne Zeman of Irving Press Publishers, I would not have been able to navigate the publishing process. Jennifer Wilkins of the Cornell Cooperative Extension gave generously of her time and contributed two important chapters. Roger Blobaum, Vance Young of the New Jersey Department of Agriculture's Jersey Fresh Program, and Hilary Baum of Windows on the World also made significant contributions. Pat Mikell and Sue Loden of Kings Super Markets, along with Diane Carr at the Bernards Inn and Faith Bahadurian of Encore Books, provided ongoing affirmation and support for this project.

Ed Lidzbarski, Torrey Reade, Michael Rassweiler, and Pam Flory for taking time out from the fields to contribute their thoughts on farming in New Jersey.

I am deeply indebted to those who worked behind the scenes to make this book possible. To Anna Sprague, whose work I have admired for years, for creating illustrations and a cover design that set the perfect tone for the book. To Wendy Rickard Bollentin for her editing skills, her ability to bring order to the chaos of my mind and office, and her unwavering faith in my ability to make this book happen. To Palmer Uhl for her technical and moral support. To Paula Plantier whose incredible attention to detail allowed me to sleep well at night. To Martha Hester Stafford for applying her years of experience as a cooking instructor to the awesome task of recipe editing and for sharing in the joys and anguish of working on a project like this with a toddler in the house. And to Joseph George, who appeared at just the right moment to take on the job of recipe tester—a job he carried out with grace and good humor.

Finally, I extend special thanks to Alice Waters for sharing her vision of a world made better by the communal breaking of bread.

Fran McManus

My staff, including Emily Brown Rosen, Michele Bassler, Leslie Van Hoose, and Cynthia Beloff, provided the necessary support and attention to help this project along. NOFA-NJ board president Leonard Pollara offered continued support throughout the process. His commitment, wit, wisdom, and perseverance have sustained both me and NOFA-NJ in countless ways. I also thank the entire NOFA-NJ board for its faith in and support of the project.

The expression *Organic Garden State* was created by the Whole Earth Center in Princeton, New Jersey. I thank Hella McVay and the Board of Trustees of the Whole Earth Center for allowing us to adopt it and for the center's ongoing commitment to NOFA-NJ and New Jersey's organic farmers.

Most important, this guide would never have been produced if not for the great talents and abilities of its editor and designer, Fran McManus, who pulled together the pieces, put together an amazing team of recipe testers and editors, and managed the endless details. Her vision, organization, and clarity are unsurpassed. And there isn't anyone else I know who could have ever pulled this off. Thank you, Fran.

Finally, I offer my sincere appreciation to the growing number of consumers who know that nothing beats the taste of local, seasonal, organic produce. Let's work together to make New Jersey the Organic Garden State.

Donna Batcho
Executive Director
NOFA-NJ

table of contents

foreword

All good cooking depends on the wholeness of living systems. For food truly worth the eating, there must, of course, be an understanding between the people who are cooking and the people who are being fed, and there must also be an impassioned collaboration between those who cook and those who produce the ingredients. But perhaps most of all, there must be an organic partnership between the producer and Nature—a partnership that sustains both land and people.

In that spirit, at my restaurant Chez Panisse, in Berkeley, California, we endeavor to serve nothing but the finest and freshest raw materials, cooked honestly and simply. And we try to guarantee that our ingredients are not only local and absolutely fresh but certified as organically grown, too. Why? Partly because of my own New Jersey roots.

When I was growing up in Chatham, New Jersey, we had an organic victory garden at our house, long before it was generally known how dangerous and shortsighted it was to grow food in any other way. I loved our garden. It was the site of some of my earliest, most formative sensory experiences: I'll never forget smelling flowers with my mother when I was still a toddler; and when I was four, I won our town's Fourth of July costume competition dressed up as the Queen of the Garden, bedecked with radish and pepper bracelets and wearing an asparagus skirt and a wreath of strawberries.

It was prolific, our backyard garden, and my mother really cooked from it, too: sweet corn, tomatoes, rhubarb, apples. I can still smell some of the wonderful things she made. Because I was so young, I suppose, I remember it as being huge, an acre or more, but it can't have been. Perhaps it was half that. Even so, I always had my own little corner of it and planted things on my own: great tomatoes, like Big Boys and Better Boys, and beans. I've always loved beans. I even used to love the frozen ones.

My childhood experience with food has been basic, but my adolescent experience felt wonderfully exotic. I was nineteen, I was in France, and it was as if I had never tasted anything before. It was that impressionable time of life, when the experiences you have can change you forever. In Paris in the '60s, there were still actual neighborhood farmers markets where one-star chefs shopped every morning. Outside Paris the daily markets were even more intimate, with produce right out of the people's gardens.

So much was new to me. New varieties, for example, not just the iceberg and romaine lettuce I'd grown up with, but the tender, butter lettuces and multicolored oak-leaf types, too, and salad greens that were completely new to me, like mâche and rocket. I'd never had frisée (curly endive) before, either, and I can still taste that first frisée salad, served warm with little lardons of French bacon. And the green beans, so delicate and tiny—nothing like our New Jersey beans had been. These were a revelation. The parade of French vegetables was endless. The only things that didn't change were simplicity and freshness.

When I started Chez Panisse, I knew I wanted to serve food as pure and freshly harvested as I'd had in New Jersey and as various and as beautifully prepared as I'd had in France. That meant hewing to a couple of simple maxims: Start with the ingredients first, and buy only from the people who are taking care of the land for the future. In other words, what's best right now in the garden? or at the farmers market? or at the farm stand? and was it organically grown?

After more than 25 years, we still start with those questions—the same ones consumers everywhere should be asking. We're particularly lucky at Chez Panisse, because we have our own full-time, professional forager, whose job is to be the liaison between the cooks and all our purveyors. He researches the sources and tells the cooks what the best available ingredients are at that moment of the year; only then do we compose our menus. Thanks to this collaboration between our cooks and our local organic farmers and our forager, we can serve tomatoes that have been delivered on the very day when the sweetness and the acid are in perfect balance and their texture is like silk—and we can boast that we don't bother serving fresh tomatoes at all during the other nine months of the year.

The guidebook you're holding right now gives Garden State consumers the same guidance we get from our forager, and it shows how New Jerseyans can find produce every bit as good as—or better than—anything that's grown in California or France. It's both a guidebook and a cookbook, and it will inspire you to demand nothing but the best. This book offers convincing, urgent reasons why you should support organic growers—and tells you how. With its help, you'll soon be eating with the seasons, and buying and cooking the freshest local produce at its peak. And you'll be joining a passionate collaboration to help build a viable and sustainable future—for my old home state, New Jersey, and for our old home planet, Earth.

Alice Waters
Berkeley, California
November, 1997

introduction

Eating Fresh from the Organic Garden State is a response to the many requests we at NOFA-NJ receive from local residents who want to know about organic agriculture and where to buy locally grown organic products. More than that, it is intended to help shape new attitudes about the power of organic produce and other products to improve our diets, our economy, our communities, and our planet. Within these pages you will hear from NOFA-NJ-certified farmers about the importance of preserving farming in New Jersey. You will hear from some of the area's most exciting chefs, whose outstanding recipes prove, once and for all, that organic foods need not be quirky, tasteless, or dull. Most important, you will learn what organic agriculture is, why it is important, and how you can support it.

New Jersey has a unique agricultural heritage, and we all have a stake in preserving and nurturing it. The food choices we make every day affect the future viability of agriculture in this part of the country. The nickname the Garden State is not a misnomer; it is a recognition of the unique growing conditions that produce some of the nation's tastiest and highest-quality organic and conventional crops.

Each year, the amount of acreage devoted to organic farming increases, and yet it is still difficult to find and purchase local organic products in season. The rising demand continues to exceed the limited supply. This guide is intended to explore the ways consumers can help ensure the growth of organic agriculture in New Jersey.

Organic farms are a natural fit for New Jersey, and they are an essential part of NOFA-NJ's vision for the future of New Jersey agriculture. Many organic farmers are first-time farmers. They are reclaiming former farms and farmland and contributing to a revitalized agricultural economy. Nestled between Philadelphia and New York, New Jersey is home to a highly educated and discerning consumer base. By raising the awareness of the population, we hope to make New Jersey a national model for the long-term viability of organic farming in densely populated areas.

Farming in general, and organic farming in particular, are not easy occupations. The pressure to develop open space and the high cost of preserving farmland in New Jersey present countless challenges to those who want to farm

N·O·F·A

ORGANIC

NORTHEAST FARMING

ASSOCIATION

NEW·JERSEY

NOFA-NJ is a nonprofit membership organization that promotes a system of local food production based on the principles of organic agriculture. Members include both farmers and nonfarmers who want to support the growth of organic agriculture in New Jersey and eastern Pennsylvania. NOFA-NJ certifies farms in New Jersey and eastern Pennsylvania.

organically. The growing season in New Jersey is short—four to six months at best—and too often New Jersey farmers need to compete with out-of-state growers whose large, conventional farms benefit from the economies of scale inherent in mass-production farming methods. That means that while New Jersey tomatoes are growing in abundance during the month of August, it is more than likely that the ones you find in your supermarket at that time are shipped in from out of state.

Without the support of consumers like you, New Jersey agriculture—and organic farming specifically—will not survive. What can you do to protect this important part of our state's economy? As this guide points out, you can pay attention to what you purchase and the food choices you make. Ask for New Jersey–grown organic products where you shop and where you dine, especially from June through November, when the growing season is at its peak. If you live in a municipality that preserves farmland, find out if that farmland is being farmed. It doesn't help to preserve farmland without the farming; they must go hand in hand. The New Jersey Department of Agriculture's Farm Link program links farmers with farmland. Make sure your farmland preservation committee adds this important step to its farmland preservation plan.

You can support your local farmers by buying their products, even if those products aren't organic. Tell them you would prefer organically grown products. There is always the hope they may eventually try it.

It is a big job growing an Organic Garden State, and we each have a role in making it happen. One of the most important steps you can take is to join NOFA-NJ. A membership application is enclosed in this guide along with contact information. By making a few changes in what you purchase and where you shop and by joining our community of organic-agriculture supporters, you cast your vote for a healthier state and a healthier planet. We'll be sure to let agricultural leaders, policy makers, and educators in New Jersey know where you stand.

We hope you enjoy *Eating Fresh from the Organic Garden State* and that it provides you with much food for thought. Your comments and feedback are welcome. Thank you for your support of local organic agriculture.

Donna Batcho
Pennington, New Jersey
November, 1997

SECTION 1

IN SECTION ONE WE EXPLAIN HOW A FARM BECOMES A *certified organic* FARM. AND WE TAKE A LOOK AT THE JOYS OF EATING LOCALLY GROWN *seasonal* PRODUCE. WE ALSO TAKE A TRIP OVERSEAS TO HEAR ABOUT *food miles* FROM A BRITISH GROUP THAT IS TRYING TO REDUCE THE DISTANCE THAT FOOD TRAVELS.

FEW PEOPLE WILL DENY THE PLEASURES OF DINING ON EXOTIC CUISINE. BUT IT IS OUR HOPE THAT THIS GUIDE WILL INSPIRE YOU TO SUPPORT YOUR *local growers* AND TO ADD MORE SEASONAL, LOCAL, ORGANIC PRODUCE TO YOUR DIET.

or·gan·ic

adj.\ 1. an ecological production management system that promotes and enhances biodiversity, biological cycles, and soil biological activity 2. based on minimal use of off-farm inputs and on management practices that restore, maintain, and enhance ecological harmony: *organic farming*

by Michele Bassler
NOFA-NJ Organic
Certification Program
and
Fran McManus

WHAT DOES CERTIFIED ORGANIC MEAN?

In its purest form, organic farming means more than simply farming without chemicals. It is a system of farming that works to improve the land's fertility by using natural, restorative methods rather than chemically formulated fertilizers. Organic farmers build healthy, fertile, living soil in a number of ways. By planting cover crops and green manures, they add essential nutrients to their soil. By rotating crops, their soil is replenished, pests are discouraged, and nutrient depletion is minimized. Composted plant and animal wastes are introduced to keep soil rich in organic matter and teeming with life. To prevent disease and pests, organic farmers use methods that improve air circulation, water drainage, and the structure of the soil and they select plant varieties that do well under the conditions that exist on their farms.

Certification is the most reliable way to assure the public that products labeled organic and organically grown are just that. When a grower or processor is certified organic, a public or private third-party organization such as the New Jersey chapter of the Northeast Organic Farming Association (NOFA-NJ) verifies that the grower or processor either meets or exceeds strict standards that preclude the use of synthetic chemical inputs.

To be labeled NOFA-NJ Certified Organic, a product must be grown and handled according to strict standards.

- The land on which organic food is grown must have had no synthetic fertilizers or pesticides applied for three years prior to certification.

- Farmers and processors must keep detailed records of methods and materials used, and they must reapply for certification every year.

- All farmers and processors must submit to an annual on-site inspection to ensure they are in compliance with NOFA-NJ's organic certification standards.

HOW DOES A FARM BECOME CERTIFIED BY NOFA-NJ?

To become certified, NOFA-NJ farmers must undergo a rigorous evaluation and certification process. Here is a look at that process.

Step 1. *Purchase a copy of NOFA-NJ's organic standards and an application for certification.* The organic standards are updated annually and are designed to improve, replenish, and

Organic Is More Than Produce

Although this book spotlights produce, organic agriculture in New Jersey is not confined to the production of seasonal vegetables. Some organic farms in the Garden State produce certified meat and medicinal herbs. NOFA-NJ's organic growers also produce nonfood items like hay, wool, and nursery products.

Unlike many farmers to the north of us in New York and New England, who must cope with steeply sloping fields, thin rocky topsoil, and harsh weather conditions, New Jersey farmers are fortunate to have land that can be adapted to a wide variety of agricultural uses. Along with fruits and vegetables, some farmers raise corn, wheat, oats, soybeans, and barley, which are used for feeding both humans and livestock. Because they graze our less-than-prime land, the raising of animals makes good use of land that is not suited to crop production. And our ability to raise grain means that, unlike many farmers

(continued next page)

maintain soil fertility, reduce the use of fossil fuels, encourage the use of local resources, promote biodiversity and stability of the farm ecosystem, ensure that livestock conditions are humane, and maintain a positive, healthy relationship between the farmer and the natural environment. Applications are available in the winter and are due in early spring. Application fees start at $285 and are based on a sliding scale determined by the farmer's gross sales of certified organic farm products.

Step 2. *Complete the certification application.* NOFA-NJ's certification application seeks to establish a general overview of a farm's history and condition. It ascertains the depth of the farmer's knowledge of organic farming practices and identifies potential contamination from off-site sources. The application requires specific details on issues such as:

- the management history of fields and farms, including soil fertility and pest control methods
- how the farmer maintains a satisfactory distance between organic fields and conventional farming operations or other potential sources of contamination, such as sprayed roadsides
- the type of products to be raised
- the farmer's plans for labeling products and for differentiating certified organic products from conventionally grown products that the farmer may also grow or sell
- the farmer's plans for building and managing soil fertility
- the type of equipment the farmer plans to use and, if applicable, how equipment used for applying chemicals that don't meet NOFA-NJ's organic standards will be cleaned
- how storage facilities for equipment, materials, and crops will be managed
- the location of ponds or streams used for irrigation
- where seed and seedlings are purchased and whether those sources meet NOFA-NJ's requirements for untreated seeds, certified organic seedlings, and non–genetically manipulated plant varieties
- the farmer's plans for controlling pests and diseases
- the results of tests to determine soil condition and health
- the results of nitrate and coliform bacteria water tests to help ensure food safety—if the farmer plans to wash produce prior to sale

*in the Northeast, we do not
need to import supplemental
feed. Animal manure can be
recycled to fertilize other
crops on our farms, and
many animals can be
fattened on hay, a crop
which is also an excellent
organic soil improver.*

*Crop diversity contributes
to the health of our farms,
building soils and prevent-
ing disease. A wide variety
of locally grown organic
crops also contribute to the
health of people living in the
Garden State. We do not
live by vegetables alone.
Check the farmer directory
in the back of this book or
call NOFA-NJ for names of
local farmers who produce
organic grains and meat.*

Torrey Reade
Neptune Farm
Salem, New Jersey
NOFA-NJ certified

*Editor's note: NOFA-NJ certifies
farms where beef, poultry, and pork
products are raised. The U.S.
Department of Agriculture,
however, forbids the labeling of any
of these products as organic.
Therefore, the only way to ensure
that meat products are raised
organically is to see the farmer's
certificate of certification. The
Organic Foods Production Act
(see next page) does contain
guidelines for the raising of meat
products, and its implementation
will allow for the labeling of these
products as organic.*

- the manner in which livestock will be housed and managed and the sources of certified organic feed
- the construction and management of greenhouses

Step 3. *Submit to an on-site farm inspection.* During the late spring or summer, an independent inspector visits the farm and meets with the farmer. The inspector checks the fields and crops, reviews the farmer's records, confirms the infor- mation on the application, and notes whether or not the farmer is following NOFA-NJ standards.

Step 4. *Undergo certification board review.* The inspector issues a report to a certification board of approximately eight volunteers representing a variety of backgrounds in agricul- ture, academia, and government. The board reviews each application and makes a decision on whether to approve for certification. If no synthetic pesticides or fertilizers have been used for at least 36 months prior to the request for certification, it is possible the crop will be certified the first year of application. If not, the farm is certified as Transitional Organic—a designation it maintains until the 36-month period has passed.

Step 5. *Gain the right to label products as certified organic.* Once the fields are certified, crops from those fields may be labeled NOFA-NJ Certified Organic or NOFA-NJ Certified Transitional Organic and sold to consumers, restaurants, wholesale distributors, retailers, packing houses, and proces- sors. A certificate is issued to the farm stating which fields are certified and the dates of the certification period. The certificate is usually on display at the farmer's stand. If not, farmers who are selling their products as certified organic should be able to produce their certificate upon request.

Step 6. *Apply for recertification.* Both certified organic and transitional farmers must reapply each year and are required to keep detailed records throughout the year. Application fees for recertification start at $235 and are based on a sliding scale determined by the farmer's gross sales of certi- fied organic farm products. The fees cover only a part of the cost of certification. The remainder is subsidized through donations and contributions to NOFA-NJ.

ORGANIC PROCESSING AND HANDLING

Once certified organic products leave the farm, care must be taken to ensure that their integrity is not compromised.

Farmers who are eligible for certification include those who grow crops such as fruits, vegetables, herbs, grains, sprouts, mushrooms, and ornamental plants or who raise livestock for the production of meat, eggs, milk, or fiber.

Processors who are eligible for certification include those who change the appearance or physical state of a product by baking, churning, cooking, cutting, dehydrating, drying, eviscerating, extracting, fermenting, freezing, grinding, heating, milling, mincing, packaging, preserving, separating, or smoking.

Handlers do not change the appearance or physical state of a product. They include brokers, commission merchants, distributors, and packers. In some cases, handlers who do not take legal title to a product do not need to be certified.

Retailers, such as supermarkets and natural foods stores, are not required to be certified under the federal law but may choose to be certified as a further guarantee to their customers.

Therefore, businesses and individuals who process or handle certified organic products and wish to label them as such also must be certified. This represents a tremendous commitment on the part of those businesses. They must physically separate all organic ingredients from any conventionally grown products, use approved sanitizers to clean from their production lines all residues from previously processed nonorganic products, and carefully select pest control methods within their facility to avoid contamination of organically grown products.

All handlers and processors wishing to be certified must fill out an application, pay a fee, and submit to inspection and review by the certification board. Unlike farmers, handlers and processors may apply for certification at any time. They must also follow NOFA-NJ standards that prevent contamination or mixing with noncertified food and that describe approved materials for processing aids, sanitation, and added ingredients. Thorough records must be kept to trace all organic foods back to the field. Labels must be clear to the consumer. For instance, if a processor is making sun-dried tomatoes, records must prove that the tomatoes came from a certified farm and that no synthetic chemicals were used in the drying process, and the label must adequately convey the percentage of organic ingredients. Only then can the final label read *NOFA-NJ Certified Organic*.

⚘

The Organic Foods Production Act was passed in 1990 and is now in the implementation phase. The act created the National Organic Program to establish national standards for the production and handling of foods labeled organic. Comprehensive recommendations for the content of those standards came from the National Organic Standards Board, an advisory board composed of four farmers, two handlers and/or processors, one retailer, one scientist with expertise in toxicology, ecology, or biochemistry, three consumer advocates, and three environmentalists.

The objective of the program is to minimize confusion in the marketplace and to protect against mislabeling and fraud. Private and state certification agencies will continue to serve as certifying bodies. After the Organic Foods Production Act is fully implemented, it will be a federal offense to label any product organic unless it has been certified. There will be an exemption to this rule for growers with annual sales of less than $5,000 worth of organic products.

Recent studies have found that some chemicals used in pesticides interfere with hormones and disrupt the normal growth and development of mammals, birds, reptiles, amphibians, and humans.

Source: Organic Trade Association, from Our Stolen Future by Theo Colburn. See Resources

by Fran McManus

WHY SHOULD I BUY LOCAL ORGANIC PRODUCTS?

NOFA-NJ's organic farmers work to improve the local environment and to keep their communities free from toxic agricultural chemicals. They can succeed in that mission only with the support of consumers who value both their products and their farming methods. Supporting local organic growers ensures access to the fresh, delicious, organic products so highly prized by chefs and home cooks. There are, however, other benefits to maintaining an active community of organic farmers in our state.

Protecting local farms

New Jersey's organic farms are typically small family farms that grow a variety of fruits, vegetables, grains, and animal products for local markets. Their existence plays an important role in a region that is experiencing frenetic growth, loss of farmland, and rapid suburbanization of rural areas. A thriving community of local organic farms helps ensure the continued viability of small farms, makes productive use of open land, and maintains diversity of land use in our state.

Preserving and enhancing the local environment

Organic farmers work to build healthy soil that is full of living organisms and free of toxic chemicals. Herbicides and synthetic fertilizers have been identified as major sources of the nonpoint pollution of streams and aquifers. Organic farmers use cultivation and crop rotation to eliminate weeds and apply natural materials to fertilize their soil, which helps keep unwanted chemicals out of local water systems. Many of the techniques used by organic farmers to enhance their soil also help to prevent erosion and runoff, thereby reducing the problems of sediment loading and nitrogen contamination in local streams, lakes, and rivers.

Local organic farmers conserve natural resources in other ways. By using human energy and natural fertilizers, they reduce their reliance on fossil fuels, and by composting, they turn plant and animal waste into fertilizer for next year's crops. The humus in their soil retains moisture, thereby reducing the need for irrigation. And because local organic farmers are situated close to their customers, it takes less trucking to get their products to market.

Reducing chemical pesticides in your community

Many of the pesticides now used on food crops—and approved by the U.S. Environmental Protection Agency—are classified as probable human carcinogens. Testing of chemical pesticides and studies of human and animal exposure have linked them to a variety of health problems, including some forms of cancer, impaired functioning of the immune system, neurological problems, and disruption of the hormones that regulate the body's sexual development. The farmworkers who apply these pesticides and the factory workers who manufacture them are at greatest risk because of their frequent and intense exposure. People living near farms also may be exposed to pesticide drift. Concerns have also been raised about the risk to humans who consume fruits and vegetables grown using synthetic pesticides. And because pesticides have traditionally been tested individually, little is known about the health risks created by long-term combined exposure to multiple pesticides. The risk to children is even higher. Until the passage of the 1996 Food Quality Protection Act (FQPA), acceptable pesticide residue levels were based on adult tolerances; this failed to take into account that relative to their size, children eat far more fruits and vegetables than adults and that they have faster metabolisms. In addition, children's organ systems are growing and developing and are therefore more vulnerable to toxic injury. The FQPA is being implemented now but until 2005 won't be fully applied to all pesticides currently used.

Because organic certification precludes the use of synthetic and persistent pesticides, local organic farmers reduce the risk of exposure to chemical pesticides for their workers and their communities. They provide fresh fruits and vegetables that are grown without the use of synthetic pesticides and therefore have a greatly reduced chance of carrying pesticide residues.

Maintaining diversity in our food crops

Genetic diversity is how nature—and the organic farmer—protect against massive crop loss by disease or infestation. Factory farms typically plant vast acreage with genetically identical seed varieties. Those varieties are selected for qualities that make them practical for large-scale, centralized farming, such as their ability to withstand mechanical harvesting, long-distance trucking, and lengthy storage times. This means that whereas we once relied on numerous small farms growing local varieties of an assortment of crops, production of the world's food supply is now being shifted onto fewer, large farms growing fewer plant varieties. The resulting lack of genetic diversity means less choice for the consumer and causes our primary food sources to be more vulnerable to destruction by disease and pests, thereby putting the world's food supply at risk.

New Jersey's organic growers grow a variety of crops that are rotated on a regular basis. Because they are close to their customers, they are not limited to growing varieties of fruits and vegetables that ship well. Instead, they can grow antique and heirloom varieties that are chosen for their

Soil and dirt are two very different things. Dirt is an inert planting medium that holds up plants. Soil is a wonderfully dynamic, ever-changing, complex, living system of life, energy, and minerals. Soil, along with water, air, and sunlight, is one of the basic building blocks of life on earth.

From J. Howard Garrett's Organic Manual. See Resources

flavor, genetic diversity, and suitability to our climate. This gives consumers true choice in the marketplace and helps preserve genetic diversity in our food supply.

Preserving the gene pool

In an attempt to "improve" foods, scientists are now swapping genetic material from bacteria, animals, and plants. On supermarket shelves are a variety of products that have been produced with this new technology—most without any labeling that identifies them as genetically engineered. That may include squash and tomatoes that have had genetic materials from viruses added to delay their ripening, thicken their skins, or increase their resistance to plant viruses; corn and potatoes that have had bacterial toxins added to their genetic codes; and thousands of other products—from baby foods to breads—containing soybeans that have been genetically altered to withstand high doses of herbicides. On the horizon are many more genetically engineered foods such as fast-growing salmon, apples that don't brown when peeled, and lentils that won't give you gas.

Although some hail genetic engineering as the salvation of the world's food supply, many scientists, environmentalists, and consumer groups stand in fierce opposition to those techniques. Little is known about the long-term health effects of eating genetically engineered foods or the chain reactions that could be set off by releasing altered genetic material into the environment.

NOFA-NJ's certification guidelines prohibit the use of genetically engineered products of any kind. The label is your guarantee that you will not be made an unwilling participant in the mass food-safety trial of these experimental products, and it preserves your right to make informed choices about the foods you eat.

Simplifying your life

Many of the so-called scientific advances taking place in modern agribusiness have sparked heated debates in the courts and the press over the ethics and safety of tampering with food production. Consider foods that undergo exposure to radiation to kill mold, bacteria, and insects. Or swapping genetic materials to create "superior" food products. Or injecting cows with a genetically engineered growth hormone to increase their milk production. Sound appealing? If not, you may have trouble identifying the products created in this way because the federal government usually does not require special labeling to differentiate them. Fortunately, we make it easy for consumers who wish to avoid those products; just look for the label *NOFA-NJ Certified Organic.*

WHAT SHOULD I BUY—AND AVOID—WHEN ORGANIC IS NOT AVAILABLE?

The bottom line is clear: you're better off eating fruits and vegetables *with* pesticides than not eating fruits and vegetables. But it's still useful to know which ones are more likely to contain pesticide residues.

"Strawberries are by far the most contaminated fruit or vegetable," says Richard Wiles, vice president of research at the Environmental Working Group (EWG). The Washington, D.C., consumer group analyzed U.S. Food and Drug Administration (FDA) inspection data from 1992 and 1993 to rate 42 fruits and vegetables. The EWG considered both the levels of pesticides found on them and how toxic those pesticides are.

The FDA detected a total of 30 different pesticides on different batches of strawberries, for example. Seventy percent of all strawberries contained at least one pesticide, and 36 percent contained two or more. Strawberries also were laced with the highest average levels of endocrine disruptors, which can mimic or interfere with hormones. Other surprises:

1. Many of the best-for-you fruits and vegetables—like cauliflower, sweet potatoes, cabbage, blueberries, carrots, bananas, and broccoli—were among the *least* likely to be contaminated.

2. Domestic cherries were almost three times more likely to contain pesticide residues than imported cherries.

3. Imported cantaloupes (available January through May) and grapes (available January through June) were more likely to be contaminated than U.S.-grown cantaloupes and grapes.

The EWG's complete report, *A Shopper's Guide to Pesticides in Produce*, is available on the World Wide Web at www.ewg.org.

Copyright 1997 CSPI/adapted from the **Nutrition Action Health Letter** • 1875 Connecticut Ave., N.W., Suite 300 • Washington, D.C. 20009-5728. $24 for 10 issues

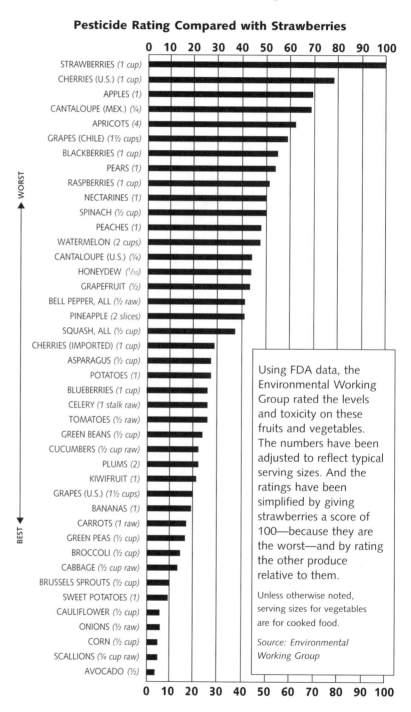

Pesticide Rating Compared with Strawberries

Using FDA data, the Environmental Working Group rated the levels and toxicity on these fruits and vegetables. The numbers have been adjusted to reflect typical serving sizes. And the ratings have been simplified by giving strawberries a score of 100—because they are the worst—and by rating the other produce relative to them.

Unless otherwise noted, serving sizes for vegetables are for cooked food.

Source: Environmental Working Group

lo·cal

\adj.\ originating in your neighborhood, town, state, or region of the country

A community food system is a collaborative effort in a particular place to build more locally based, self-reliant food economies. Community food systems seek comprehensive solutions to food and agricultural problems by involving community members in promoting community food security; farmland preservation; local, direct marketing; community economic development; a stable base of family farmers that use production practices that are less chemical and energy intensive; improved working and living conditions for farm labor; and public policies and planning that encourage a more sustainable food system.[1]

by Jennifer L. Wilkins Ph.D., R.D.
Senior Extension Associate
Division of
Nutritional Sciences
Cornell University

WHY SHOULD I BUY FROM LOCAL GROWERS?

Much of what Americans eat has little if any connection to their surrounding landscape. The combination of new technology and highly advanced transportation systems makes it easy to enjoy a truly global diet. The Rodale Institute estimates that food consumed in the United States travels an average of 1,300 miles from point of production to point of consumption.[2] The joy of eating locally grown, seasonal produce has given way to the luxury of eating whatever we crave, whenever we crave it, regardless of how far it must travel. Even though today we enjoy a variety of foods throughout the year, there are compelling reasons we should take another look at—and another bite of!— what is produced and processed locally. Fear not, however; this is not a call for your total diet to be planned according to what can be grown and processed within a 50-mile radius of your home. It is an invitation to enhance the local character of your cuisine, thereby ensuring a future for agriculture in your community.

Keeping the local economy and community strong

The fact is, our daily food choices can have a significant impact on our local economy. Buying locally grown and processed foods supports the complex food system that exists in our area and helps maintain both economic stability and food security in our region. When you consider the many steps and businesses involved in getting food from farm to table—crops must be planted and harvested and the food then processed, transported, packaged, stored, and marketed—you can begin to understand how food itself contributes to a growing, healthy local economy.

Buying locally helps achieve what is called a community food system (see sidebar). The act of supporting regional farms and regional food processors benefits not only farmers but an area's entire economy as well. Studies show that rural communities that have many family farms have healthier economies than those that don't. In those areas, the loss of a single farm can mean the loss of three to five other rural jobs, with fewer farms buying feed, seed, and fertilizer. Such losses also have an impact on other local businesses. Consider this: the loss of six farms in a single area can result in one failed rural business.[3] Maintaining a diverse agriculture nearer to where consumers live helps strengthen local communities.

Preserving local farmland

When we purchase foods produced outside our region, we weaken our own regional economy. The farms that dot the northeastern U.S. landscape help keep it healthy and vibrant. In a recent study of consumers in the Northeast, 98 percent agreed it's important to keep farming viable in the region; 97 percent said they felt that buying local produce is an effective way to do that. Yet according to the Census of Agriculture, the Northeast is losing farms at an alarming rate: about 3,300 each year. Although farms fail for a variety of reasons, they stand little chance of survival without the strong support of local consumers.

Protecting natural resources

Today's intensive global transport of food requires a complex infrastructure that carries a hefty environmental cost. From food processing, extensive use of refrigerants, and development of travel-grade packaging to the manufacture and maintenance of large, long-haul trucks, food shipment is a resource-intensive aspect of our food system. In addition, a considerable amount of energy is used for transporting fresh produce great distances. And although the price of fuel is low enough to make it economical to ship food across the country—and around the world—the environmental costs, such as air pollution, oil spills, and damaged roadways, are rarely taken into account.

The joy of eating local foods in season

There are other, less tangible benefits to eating foods that are grown regionally and in season. You become much more aware of the seasons, the weather, and your area's agricultural cycles. Eating this way also leads to a heightened sense of excitement and anticipation as the season for your favorite local produce arrives. Once you've tasted a juicy, local, vine-ripened tomato at the peak of the season, it may be hard to swallow the pale, hard tomatoes offered in supermarkets in the middle of winter. If you are like most consumers, you know that local fruits and vegetables are fresher and tastier than produce shipped from distant states and countries.

But can one's nutrient requirements be met by eating a local diet? Yes, and more than adequately. By means of the *Northeast Regional Food Guide*, daily menus of two meals a day for fall, winter, and spring were designed and analyzed for their nutrient content. Results indicated that diets based

The Jersey Fresh program is an advertising and promotional program designed to make consumers aware of the many farm products produced in New Jersey. Farmers interested in using the Jersey Fresh logo on their packaging must register with the New Jersey Department of Agriculture. All produce packed under the Jersey Fresh logo must meet certain grade standards and is subject to inspection by department officials.

New Jersey ranks fourth in the United States in production of peaches, fifth in spinach, and seventh in sweet corn.

FOOTNOTES

[1] Definition developed by Dave Campbell at the University of California Sustainable Agriculture Research & Education Program.

[2] Rodale Institute, 1981. *Empty Breadbasket: The Coming Challenge to America's Food Supply and What We Can Do about It.* The Cornucopia Project. Rodale Press, Emmaus, Pennsylvania.

[3] D. Pimentel, 1990. "Environmental and Social Implications of Waste in U.S. Agriculture and Food Sectors." *Journal of Agricultural Ethics*, p. 7.

[4] J. L. Wilkins and J. D. Gussow, 1997. "Regional Dietary Guidance: Is the Northeast Nutritionally Complete?" *Conference Proceedings for the International Conference on Agricultural Production and Nutrition*, Boston, Massachusetts, March 19–21, 1997.

on what is or could be available from our region supplied at least 100 percent of the Recommended Dietary Allowance (RDA) for an average adult female aged 25 to 50.[4]

HOW DO I BECOME A MORE REGIONAL EATER?

As with any personal change, becoming a regional and seasonal eater will be easier—and more lasting—if you start gradually. The most difficult part is remembering to think about it when you shop. Here are some tips to get you started:

- When choosing produce in your supermarket or food store, notice where it was grown. This may sound simple, but not many people do it. If you have the option of buying a locally grown item, do so. Remember: how you choose to spend your food dollars makes a difference.

- If you live in the Northeast, many juices and ciders are made from fruits grown in the area—particularly cranberry, grape, and apple. Make an effort to find juices and ciders from regional sources. Supermarket managers are becoming aware that promoting local food products is good business, so it may become easier to identify local foods.

- If you're not sure where the produce you're buying was grown, find out. Ask your supermarket manager to post signs. Let the manager know you prefer fruits and vegetables that are locally grown. Similarly, get into the habit of asking farm stand proprietors if the produce they sell is their own. If not, find out where it's grown.

- Become a member of a community-supported farm. Picking up your weekly share from a Community Supported Agriculture (CSA) farm is one of the best ways to learn firsthand what is grown locally and when it's available. And many of the CSA farms offer recipes, so you can also improve your local culinary vocabulary.

- When you eat in a restaurant, order foods that are—or can be—grown or produced in the region. Some restaurants now specialize in creating menus based on local foods as well as those produced using organic, sustainable methods. Make it a point to support those restaurants.

- Get involved in food planning committees at schools and other institutions in your area. Help identify local and regional alternatives to current purchases.

food miles

\n.\ a unit of measurement used to determine the distance that food travels from farm to table

Although it refers to issues facing food producers in the United Kingdom, we have included this article because the concerns raised about the problems of long-distance food transport are ones that we also face in New Jersey and the rest of the United States. See Resources for more information about the Sustainable Agriculture Food and Environment Alliance and its Food Miles campaign.

by Angela Paxton
The SAFE Alliance
London

WHAT ARE THE ECONOMIC, SOCIAL, AND ENVIRONMENTAL EFFECTS OF SHIPPING FOODS OVER GREAT DISTANCES?

In the United Kingdom, very few of our foods come from local producers. Apples from New Zealand and prawns from Bangladesh, for example, travel an average of 13,000 miles to our supermarkets, where we pick and choose from the world's food store. Few of us question the social and ecological impacts of this phenomenon, such as pollution, excess packaging, loss of biodiversity, and diminished food security in developing countries. The Sustainable Agriculture Food and Environment (SAFE) Alliance's Food Miles campaign aims to raise awareness of those issues and offers solutions for increasing consumption and availability of local and regional foods.

Transport

Excessive and unnecessary transport of food, particularly via road and air freight, contributes to a wide range of environmental and social hazards, including air and noise pollution, acid rain, and health problems such as respiratory illness. Yet food is being transported over greater and greater distances each year. Between 1979 and 1994, the average distance food traveled increased by more than 50 percent, even as the amount of food transported remained the same. Nearly a third of the overall increase in freight transport in the U.K. during that period was attributable to food, drink, and tobacco—most of which was food—more than to any other major commodity group.

International food miles also are on the rise: the amount of food that travels by air to the U.K., such as fresh fruit and vegetables, more than doubled during the 1980s. Air travel consumes 37 times more fuel per metric ton than ground transportation. Pollutants emitted by air freight occur mainly at high altitudes, where they do more damage to the ozone layer than do those emitted at ground level.

Preservation

Food that travels great distances requires extra packaging, pesticide treatment, and processing to help preserve it during its long-distance trek around the globe. Citrus fruits that travel from Brazil to our supermarket shelves, for example, may endure many treatments of fungicides and waxes. Pesticides often are applied on fruits and vegetables after harvest to extend shelf life and prevent damage in transport.

Every year about 100 million–150 million pounds of pesticides that cannot be used in the United States are exported for use in other countries. These pesticides have been banned or not registered for use in the United States because they may have adverse effects on human and animal health or because their level of destructiveness to the environment is too high. Such chemicals continue to be manufactured in pesticide factories in the United States, where plant workers and residents of the surrounding communities are exposed to them.

Then the pesticides are shipped overseas, where farmworkers are exposed to them when they are applied to crops. Runoff from the fields results in contaminated water supplies, drift from spraying pollutes the air, and farmworkers bring home pesticides clinging to their clothes. Animals eat the grain and grass that have been sprayed, and the people of the country eat that livestock and the sprayed produce and grain.

Finally, food treated with these chemicals—which the U.S. Environmental Protection Agency has not approved for use—is then imported back into the United States to be sold at grocery stores nationwide.

(continued next page)

Fresh, locally produced foods escape this kind of treatment because of the shorter distance and shelf life between farmer and consumer.

Packaging

Up to two-thirds of domestic packing in the U.K. is used for food and drink products. Long-distance transport of food and drink, which take both the food and its packaging far from its source, makes it difficult to reduce and reuse.

Biodiversity

Farmers are growing fewer varieties of crops and are having to meet increasingly strict criteria for produce, particularly when the crop is for sale in distant markets either in other parts of the country or overseas. Farmers and growers supplying supermarkets, for example, have to concentrate on appearance, uniformity, and travel and storage qualities, especially long shelf life. As a result, local crop varieties adapted to the regional climate and conditions are being replaced by a few commercial varieties.

The reduction of biodiversity makes crops more vulnerable to pests and disease. Increased applications of chemicals such as pesticides are then needed to keep the crop free of infestation. And the pests and disease quickly become resistant to new chemicals, setting the farmer on a chemical treadmill.

Farming

Farming is becoming an increasingly insecure profession as long-distance trade and transport of food become the norm. For example, many U.K. salad growers faced ruin in 1994 because of competition from imports of lettuces, tomatoes, and cucumbers, sold at prices far below those that could reasonably have been set for home-produced items.

Developing countries

The ability of countries to feed themselves may be hindered when the best agricultural land is used for production of crops for export, typically to richer countries. For example, Brazil is the third-largest exporter of food and agricultural products in the world, yet two out of three Brazilians do not have enough to eat. The people producing export crops

This trail of dangerous pesticides is called the circle of poison. What can be done to break the circle of poison? Prohibit the export of pesticides that are not registered for domestic use or that do not have a food tolerance, that are not registered for food use and that would be exported for use on food, and that have had the majority (by volume) of registrations canceled. Temporary exemptions would be permitted for emergencies such as famine or communicable disease.

Permit governments of importing countries to refuse the import of especially hazardous pesticides. Such import refusals must be based on health and environmental concerns, not trade barriers.

Automatically revoke tolerances for pesticide residues on food of those pesticides no longer registered in the United States.

What can you do? Buy food grown in the United States. Ask your grocer to sell organic produce and to label the country of origin of all produce stocked. Ask your congressional representatives to support legislation to stop the export of banned pesticides. Contact Pesticide Action Network or the Foundation for Advancements in Science and Education for more information on the circle of poison.

Produced by the National Campaign for Pesticide Policy Reform using information provided by Greenpeace

usually are poor and working for low pay in difficult conditions. Food and agricultural products usually are exported to pay off debts and purchase imports rather than to improve the lives of ordinary people.

Reducing food miles

Reducing the need to transport food is the most effective way of reducing food miles. Increasing local and regional self-reliance would go a long way toward reducing waste of energy and resources and increasing biodiversity in farming, and it should help provide greater food security as well as more sustainable livelihoods for farmers both in the U.K. and overseas.

FOOD FOR THOUGHT ON FLOWERS FOR YOUR TABLE

With their irresistible colors and intoxicating aromas, fresh-cut flowers make a beautiful addition to any table in your house. When choosing flowers, however, be as discriminating as you would when choosing vegetables and fruits. They should be locally grown, fresh, and free of harmful chemicals. The flower business lends itself to heavy applications of pesticides to accommodate people's taste for perfect-looking flowers. Those shipped from other countries often are heavily sprayed with pesticides and fumigants to keep them fresh. Remember: Flowers are like vegetables. If the soil they are grown in is healthy, they in turn will be healthy and less likely to be affected by pests and disease.

Fresh-cut flowers are usually found at farm stands. If you want your florists to carry local, organically grown flowers, let them know. You can choose to purchase locally grown organic flowers for the same reasons you choose locally grown organic produce: because they are grown using methods that are safe for the environment and safe for your family.

Pam Flory
Pam's Garden
*   at North Slope Farm*
Lambertville, New Jersey
NOFA-NJ certified

sea·son·al

by Jennifer L. Wilkins
Ph.D., R.D.
Senior Extension Associate
Division of
Nutritional Sciences
Cornell University

\adj.\ 1. specific to a particular place at a particular time of year 2. harvested and eaten at the peak of flavor and ripeness: *seasonal produce*

When you look at what's available in the produce department of your local supermarket on any given day, you may not be able to tell whether it's January or July. The sophisticated global sourcing capabilities that characterize the fruit and vegetable industry have made it possible to eat fresh fruits and vegetables throughout the year, regardless of the season. Produce grown thousands of miles away is shipped to our supermarkets with little thought given to how such movement of food affects local economies, the future of local farming, our natural resources, and the quality of the food we eat.

WHAT IS A SEASON?

For most of us, seasons are defined by the months and days of a calendar. In terms of agriculture, however, seasons are defined according to the first and last time frost comes to an area. The northeastern region of the United States spans several latitudes and varies in geography and climate. Spring in northern New England can begin much later than spring in the Mid-Atlantic states. The last frost date for your area—meaning the last day, on average, the temperature falls below freezing—marks the time when spring produce, which is planted in very early spring, will begin to mature and become ready for harvest. In the Northeast, as spring progresses, we look for peas, asparagus, lettuce, rhubarb, radishes, and a variety of greens. Early-maturing broccoli, cauliflower, turnips, and beets are harvested later in spring. At the time of the last frost date, when the threat of frost damage to plants ends, vegetable farmers may begin planting summer crops, such as tomatoes, corn, beans, squash, and peppers. Also at this time, farmers make their first cutting of hay and dairy cows are sent out to pasture to graze on the lush grass.

Some summer produce, such as green beans, is ready six weeks after planting. Other kinds, such as tomatoes, are ready eight or nine weeks after planting. During summer, Northeasterners enjoy a wide array of ripe fruit such as peaches, plums, cherries, melons, and berries.

The first frost, which marks the end of summer and the transition to fall, may slip by unnoticed. It may occur at night, even when daytimes are still warm. Most summer vegetables cannot survive freezing temperatures, whereas fall crops thrive in cooler weather. Fall broccoli, cabbages,

Brussels sprouts, and grapes actually get sweeter after a frost. Depending on where you live, fall produce may be available from one to several months before very cold weather sets in.

Winter produce begins to take the place of fall produce once a long stretch of severely cold weather arrives. In harsher climates, winter crops such as kale and leeks are available only the first month or two of the season. In milder climates, those more tender crops may be available throughout winter. Most winter favorites, such as potatoes, onions, carrots, cabbage, winter squash, apples, and beets, as well as less familiar vegetables, such as burdock, rutabagas, and Jerusalem artichokes, are harvested in late fall and stored throughout winter. Some crops are available from greenhouses, and there is always a wide variety of canned and frozen alternatives from which to choose. As winter ends and temperatures warm, watch out for the last frost date in spring. It's time for spring produce and the beginning of another cycle.

TIPS FOR SEASONAL EATING

Becoming a seasonal eater isn't difficult. While it may not be reasonable to convert your entire diet to local, seasonal foods, there are many small changes you can make as the calendar rolls around. Here are some ideas to help you get started.

- During summer and fall, buy produce from a local farmers market, roadside stand, or U-pick farm or choose produce identified in your supermarket or food store as locally grown.

- During the winter months, include familiar, locally grown fruits and vegetables in your diet, such as potatoes, winter squash, carrots, cabbage, onions, beets, garlic, apples, and pears.

- In the winter, try including at least two less-familiar vegetables in your diet, such as celeriac, Jerusalem artichokes, kale, parsnips, rutabagas, turnips, or kohlrabi.

- In the summer and fall, enjoy the abundance of fresh fruit and vegetables harvested in the Northeast. During the winter, when fresh produce is not available, explore the wide variety of northeastern-grown produce that is canned, frozen, dried, and stored.

The New Jersey Department of Agriculture offers several publications for those interested in locating local produce. They include:

Where to Find Pick-Your-Own Fruits and Vegetables in New Jersey

Where to Find New Jersey Apples

New Jersey Roadside and Urban Markets Directory

These publications are free of charge and can be obtained by calling the New Jersey Department of Agriculture at 609-292-8853. See Resources for more information.

Today less than 2 percent of the U.S. population live on farms. In 1930 it was 30 percent, and when the Constitution was signed it was 90 percent.

~ A new food guide, the *Northeast Regional Food Guide,* was developed by the Cornell Cooperative Extension to help consumers learn which foods are not available fresh in the Northeast during winter. Chances are, if you are like most Americans, you eat some of these foods on a regular basis. To become a more seasonal eater, start by replacing one or two nonregional foods that you eat often during winter with alternatives that are produced locally, such as celeriac for celery. If you tend to eat an imported item once a day, try cutting back to once a week. Use the *Northeast Regional Food Guide* to find nutritionally compatible substitutes that are available regionally. To order, see Resources.

~ During summer, visit a U-pick farm and pick enough to can or freeze some of what you pick. Berries are easy to freeze. Put them on a cookie sheet, and place the cookie sheet in the freezer. Once they're frozen, store them in small, airtight plastic bags in the freezer. Home-based food preservation seems to be a dying—or dead—art, but small-scale food processing is a growing phenomenon in the Northeast and may mean that in the near future it will be easier to find foods preserved from the local harvest.

Remember: Eating with the seasons helps create a stronger connection to where we live. Just as our communities are characterized by their trees, buildings, parks, rivers, and hillsides, our region has its own seasonal food supply. To eat what is locally available in season is to celebrate the magnificent bounty our region has to offer.

Jersey Fresh Availability Chart

	JAN	FEB	MAR	APR	MAY	JUN	JUL	AUG	SEP	OCT	NOV	DEC
APPLES	■	■	■	■	■	■	■	■	■	■	■	■
ASPARAGUS				■	■							
BEANS, SNAP						■	■	■	■	■		
BEETS						■	■	■	■	■	■	
BLACKBERRIES							■					
BLUEBERRIES						■	■					
BROCCOLI								■	■	■	■	■
CABBAGE						■	■	■	■	■	■	■
CANTALOUPE							■	■	■			
CAULIFLOWER					■	■	■		■			
CHERRIES						■						
CHINESE CABBAGE						■	■	■	■	■	■	
CRANBERRIES										■	■	
CUCUMBERS							■	■	■	■	■	
EGGPLANT							■	■	■	■	■	
ESCAROLE & ENDIVE						■	■	■	■	■	■	■
GRAPES									■			
GREENS & HERBS			■	■	■	■	■	■	■	■	■	■
LEEKS	■	■		■	■	■	■	■	■	■	■	■
LETTUCE, LATE SPRING					■	■						
LETTUCE, EARLY FALL										■	■	
LIMA BEANS							■	■	■			
MUSHROOMS	■	■	■	■	■	■	■		■	■	■	■
OKRA								■	■	■		
ONIONS							■	■	■	■	■	
PARSLEY					■	■	■	■	■	■	■	
PEACHES & NECTARINES							■	■	■	■		
PEARS								■	■			
PEAS					■	■						
PEPPERS							■	■	■	■		
PLUMS							■	■				
POTATOES, WHITE	■	■	■				■	■	■	■	■	■
PUMPKINS								■	■	■		
RADISHES				■	■	■	■	■	■	■		
RASPBERRIES							■	■	■	■		
SCALLIONS					■	■	■	■	■	■	■	
SPINACH					■	■			■	■	■	
SQUASH, ACORN							■	■	■	■	■	
SQUASH, BUTTERNUT	■	■	■					■	■	■	■	■
SQUASH, YELLOW						■	■	■	■			
STRAWBERRIES						■						
SWEET CORN							■	■	■	■		
SWEET POTATOES	■	■	■	■				■	■	■	■	■
TOMATOES							■	■	■	■		
TURNIPS	■	■	■			■	■	■	■	■	■	■
WATERMELONS								■	■			
ZUCCHINI						■	■	■	■	■		

| | REFRIGERATE | | FREEZE | | | PICKLE OR CAN | DRY AIR OR DRYER | ROOT CELLAR 32°–40° MOIST, DARK | DRY STORE 55° DARK | JUICE OR WINE |
	IN PLASTIC	IN VENTED PLASTIC	UNBLANCHED	BLANCHED	SAUCED					
APPLES		✓			✓	Sauce	✓	✓	✓	J, W
ASPARAGUS	✓			3 min						
BEANS, GREEN	✓			3 min		✓				
BEETS		✓				✓		✓		J
BERRIES		✓	✓			✓	✓			W
BROCCOLI	✓			3 min				✓		J
BRUSSELS SPROUTS	✓		✓	5–8 min				✓		
CABBAGE		✓		3 min				✓		J
CARROTS		✓						✓		J
CAULIFLOWER	✓			4 min						
CELERY	✓							✓		J
CHERRIES		✓	✓			✓				W
CORN, DRY	✓						✓		✓	
CORN, SWEET	✓			6–8 min						
CUCUMBERS	✓					✓			✓	
EGGPLANT	✓									
GARLIC									✓	
GREENS	✓			2–3 min						J
HERBS	✓			1 min			✓			
LEEKS		✓						✓		
LETTUCE	✓									
MELONS		✓	✓			✓	✓			J, W
MUSHROOMS	✓					✓	✓			
ONIONS									✓	
PARSNIPS		✓						✓		
PEACHES		✓	✓			✓	✓			J, W
PEARS		✓			✓	✓	✓	✓	✓	J, W
PEAS	✓			2–3 min						
PEPPERS	✓		✓				✓			
PLUMS		✓				✓				W
POTATOES		✓						✓		
RHUBARB	✓			3 min						W
RUTABAGAS		✓						✓		
SPINACH	✓			1–2 min						
SQUASH, SUMMER	✓			·						
SQUASH, WINTER									✓	
TOMATOES			✓			✓	✓		✓	
TURNIPS		✓						✓		

Preservation & Storage Guide

This chart offers suggestions for the short- and long-term storage of fruits and vegetables. By freezing, canning, and drying, you can make the most of seasonal produce and eat locally all year round. For more information on preserving foods at home, a number of good books are available, including *Stocking Up III* and *Putting Food By*. Or call the Family and Consumer Science department (formerly the Home Economics department) of your county's Cooperative Extension office. The department offers phone assistance and low-cost publications on the proper way to safely can, dry, freeze, store, and prepare foods. See Resources.

SECTION 2

IN SECTION TWO WE PRESENT A VARIETY OF *seasonal recipes* FROM AREA CHEFS WHO USE THE BEST OF OUR REGION'S BOUNTIFUL HARVEST. FROM SIMPLE TO ELABORATE, WE PRESENT AN EXCITING RANGE OF RECIPES TO ENCOURAGE YOU TO MAKE THE MOST OF EACH SEASON'S OFFERINGS. IF AN INGREDIENT IS NOT AVAILABLE FROM A LOCAL *organic farmer*, WE HOPE YOU WILL REPLACE IT WITH A LOCAL, CONVENTIONALLY GROWN PRODUCT. JUST BE SURE YOU LET THE SELLER KNOW YOU WOULD RATHER HAVE IT *grown organically*.

rec·i·pes

\n.\ a set of directions, with a list of ingredients, to help you prepare both simple and elaborate meals from fresh, seasonal ingredients

WHY CHEFS SUPPORT LOCAL ORGANIC GROWERS

Around the country, professional chefs and restaurateurs are playing a significant role in the future of ecologically sound agriculture and responsible food production. Driven by their passion for product quality and their concern for the environment, chefs are using their menus to express their commitment to local farming, they are contributing their time and talents to organizations such as the Northeast Organic Farming Association, and they are leveraging their considerable purchasing power to effect change in the marketplace.

The chefs who have provided the recipes in this book share those interests: some with an emphasis on organic products; many with a focus on local; and all with a passion for the seasonal. One of the greatest challenges facing our community today is to translate those interests into tangible economic benefits for local organic farmers.

Happily, a growing number of home cooks and professional chefs are demonstrating their commitment to ingredients that are superior in terms of flavor and freshness, diverse, and produced and distributed responsibly. That commitment is leading many to shop as close to the farm as possible: at urban farmers markets, at on-the-farm roadside stands, through CSA groups, and via other direct-buying arrangements. Others are finding local and organic products at the more traditional outlets such as health food stores, natural food markets, and the more enlightened supermarkets.

In order to strengthen and stimulate local organic farming—and to make higher-quality food available to everyone—both consumers *and* professionals should get into the habit of asking for local and organic produce wherever they shop and wherever they dine. By so doing, we all will become a part of this exhilarating and important movement in support of local, ecologically sound farming.

Hilary Baum
Windows on the World
New York

The Season's Bounty

What a pleasure it can be looking forward to each season's harvest of fresh fruits and vegetables. Although it's possible to buy almost any form of produce throughout the year—frozen, canned, or shipped across the country—nothing compares with the taste of locally grown fruits and vegetables, fresh from the market or farm stand. Try using them in season for optimum enjoyment.

The recipes in this book vary greatly in their complexity and character—a reflection of the diverse styles of the chefs who created them. They are arranged by season based on the time of year when the main ingredients are generally available from local farms. Along with each season's recipes are some simple suggestions for making the most of each season's bounty.

spring

summer

About the Ingredients Used in These Recipes

This book is intended to promote the use of locally grown products. Therefore, we asked the contributing chefs to limit the main ingredients in their recipes to those that can be raised, caught, or collected in New Jersey, Pennsylvania, and New York State. In the case of seafood, we expanded that range to include the entire Northeast.

The supply of local, organically grown products varies greatly within the states and the region. It may be difficult to find organic sources for all of the products used in these recipes. Raising the demand for locally grown organic products is one of the best ways to increase the supply, so make sure you let your local food stores and farmers know that you prefer to buy organic.

"From the time I was a boy I have been fascinated with farming. Born and raised in a small New Jersey town, my only link to agriculture was the family garden. As far as I was concerned, when I spent time in the garden I was in Kansas. Today my mother still plants the same 20'x50' plot, and when I visit and stand there among the tomato plants and beans, a wonderful peace comes over me—a feeling that lets me know that the seeds that were so gently planted in me as a child still grow strong and healthy inside me."

Ed Lidzbarski
E.R. & Son
Jamesburg, New Jersey
NOFA-NJ certified grower

spring

Asparagus and spinach come to mind first when we look for vegetables that are available at winter's end. Escarole and lettuces along with turnips, mustard greens, and bok choy are harvested soon after, as are early peas and string beans.

good ideas for spring...

Shred bok choy, and toss with minced shallots, orange juice, orange zest, mirin, and sea salt for a refreshing, nonfat salad.

Sauté onions and add sliced asparagus and Arborio rice. Stir in twice as much stock as rice, and simmer for a quick risotto.

Blanch sliced asparagus and toss with cooked penne, fresh spinach, and sun-dried tomatoes. Finish with a tasty vinaigrette made with olive oil, wine vinegar, and the juice left over from reconstituting the tomatoes.

For a refreshing spring salad, toss fresh uncooked peas and snow peas with fresh dill, nonfat yogurt, and a bit of sea salt.

Create a thyme-scented split pea soup by cooking dried split peas in water and thyme to make a thinner-than-usual soup. Stir in lots of fresh peas for a surprisingly spring touch.

Wash early spinach and without drying it, put it right into a hot sauté pan. Toss with roasted garlic for a delicious side dish. Water sautéing is a great no-fat method for cooking all kinds of spring greens.

Freshen up canned tomato–based vegetable soup by stirring in chopped escarole and elbow macaroni.

Toss fresh tarragon, thyme, oregano, parsley, and chives from the garden in soups and salads.

CAFE • COOKING SCHOOL • CATERING

Edibles...Naturally!
Princeton Junction
New Jersey
Alice Miller
Chef/Owner

Crab & Potato Salad with Young Pea Shoots

Emulsification

Emulsification of a sauce or vinaigrette occurs when a fat—such as butter or oil— is evenly dispersed in tiny droplets within a liquid with which it cannot mix.

To achieve emulsification, some kind of vigorous energy must be applied by shaking the sauce or vinaigrette in a jar or by using a whisk or blender.

In order for the emulsion to hold, you need a binder such as mustard or egg yolk.

SERVES 6

For the salad:

1½ pounds fingerling potatoes

1 pound jumbo lump crab meat

2 medium scallions, sliced thinly

3 cups (loosely packed) young pea shoots
   or baby spinach leaves

For the vinaigrette:

2 tablespoons whole grain (Pommery-style) mustard

¼ cup sherry wine vinegar

⅓ cup canola oil

¼ cup walnut or hazelnut oil

Salt and pepper to taste

1. Put whole unpeeled potatoes in a large pot. Cover with cold water by 1 inch and add a pinch of salt. Boil uncovered until the potatoes are soft. Test for doneness by inserting the blade of a paring knife into the largest potato. If there is no resistance, it is done. Strain.

2. As soon as the potatoes are cool enough to handle, slice them into ¼-inch disks, toss with scallions, crabmeat, and pea shoots or spinach.

3. To make the vinaigrette, mix together the mustard and vinegar in a small bowl. Pour in the oils in a steady stream, whisking vigorously, and season with salt and pepper to taste.

4. Toss the potatoes, crab, and scallions gently with half of the vinaigrette. Taste and add more if necessary.

5. Serve at room temperature.

THE FORRESTAL
AT PRINCETON
HOTEL & CONFERENCE CENTER

The Forrestal
Princeton, New Jersey
Yves Vacheresse
Executive Chef

Chilled Soup of Sweet Peas with Sweet Maine Shrimp, Borage Infusion & Caviar Cream

SERVES 4 TO 6

Borage Infusion (see sidebar on next page)

2 quarts *Court Bouillon* (see next page)

For the soup:

6 cups water

Salt, as needed

12 ounces sweet peas, shelled

Pepper

32 fresh sweet shrimp

For the caviar cream:

¼ cup heavy cream, chilled

2 teaspoons Osetra caviar

Sprigs of chervil, tarragon, and edible flowers such as dandelion, thyme, and pineapple sage

1. Prepare the borage infusion and court bouillon and reserve.

2. Bring the water to a boil in a 3-quart pot and add a generous pinch of salt. Prepare a bowl of ice water and set it next to the stove. Immerse the peas in the boiling water and cook until tender, about 3 to 5 minutes. Using a slotted spoon, plunge the peas into the ice bath to stop the cooking. Reserve the cooking water.

3. Place the cooked peas in a blender with 1 cup of the cooking water and purée. Gradually add more of the cooking water to bring the purée to the consistency of heavy cream. Season to taste with salt and pepper.

4. Pass the puréed peas through a fine mesh strainer or an ordinary strainer lined with 2 layers of dampened cheesecloth. Chill the strained purée in the refrigerator.

5. To prepare the shrimp, bring the court bouillon to a boil and turn down the heat. Prepare an ice water bath and set it by the stove. Place the shrimp in the hot court bouillon until they turn color, about 1 or 2 seconds.

The Ryland Inn
Whitehouse, New Jersey
Craig Shelton
Executive Chef/Proprietor

Borage Infusion

1 cup borage leaves, cleaned

½ cup extra virgin olive oil

2 tablespoons water

Salt and pepper, as needed

Bring a 2-quart pot of water to a boil and add a generous pinch of salt. Prepare a bowl of ice water and set it by the stove. Blanch the borage leaves for a few seconds until they are wilted and then plunge them into the ice bath. Drain the borage leaves and pat them dry with a paper towel.

Place the blanched borage in a blender, and with the motor running, slowly drizzle in the oil and water.

Season the mixture with salt and pepper and strain through a fine-mesh strainer or a strainer lined with two layers of dampened cheesecloth. The sauce should be dark green with a light nappé consistency.

Immediately plunge the shrimp into the ice bath. Drain and reserve.

6. To make the caviar cream, whip the cold cream until it just begins to thicken. Add a pinch of salt and pepper and continue to whip to a medium peak. Fold in the caviar and reserve.

7. To serve, pour the pea soup into individual chilled bowls. In the center of each bowl of soup, place 6 to 8 shrimp in a circle so that they overlap one another. Put a small dollop of caviar cream on the shrimp and drizzle with the borage infusion. Garnish the center of each bowl with sprigs of chervil, tarragon, and edible flowers such as dandelion, thyme, and pineapple sage.

Court Bouillon for Fish

Court bouillon literally means a short boil. It also refers to stocks that can be put together in 30 minutes and are used to poach meat, fish, and vegetables.

2 quarts water

2 tablespoons salt

1 to 2 cups white wine

2 to 4 carrots, peeled and sliced thin

2 to 3 celery stalks, sliced thin

1 medium onion, peeled and roughly chopped

1 lemon, cut in half

6 parsley stems

3 bay leaves

1 tablespoon black peppercorns

Combine all of the ingredients in a 4-quart saucepan. Bring to a boil, turn down the heat, and simmer for 25 minutes. Strain and reserve the liquid.

Striped Bass with Long Island Littlenecks & Spring Vegetables

SERVES 4

For the fish:

4 fillets of striped bass, 7 ounces each, skin on

2 tablespoons extra virgin olive oil

For the vegetables:

2 medium parsnips, peeled and diced into ¼-inch pieces

8 tablespoons unsalted butter

1 pound chanterelles, washed to remove the grit

2 tablespoons diced shallots

For the clams:

1 cup white wine

1 teaspoon chopped garlic

1 tablespoon flat-leaf parsley, chopped

24 littleneck clams, soaked in water for 1 hour and rinsed

Sea salt

Pepper

To finish:

1 small bunch thyme, chopped

1 small bunch baby arugula, washed and dried

2 tablespoons chives, chopped

1. Preheat oven to 350°F.

2. Score the skin of the striped bass with a sharp paring knife. Brush the fillets with extra virgin olive oil, cover with plastic wrap, and refrigerate while you prepare the vegetables and clams.

3. Bring a pot of water to a boil and add a generous pinch of salt. Blanch the parsnips for 30 seconds. Drain. Melt 1 tablespoon of butter in a sauté pan and sauté the parsnips for 3 to 4 minutes or until soft. Reserve on a small plate.

Windows on the World
New York
Frederic Kieffer
Private Dining Chef

4. Trim the chanterelles of any tough or discolored parts and cut into 2 pieces if large. Melt 1 tablespoon of butter in a medium sauté pan and sauté the chanterelles for 1 minute. Add 1 tablespoon of shallots and cook for another minute. Reserve in the pan.

5. In a 2-quart saucepan, bring the wine to a boil. Add the garlic, remaining shallots, parsley, and 2 tablespoons of butter. Boil for 5 minutes over high heat. Turn the heat down to medium, add the clams, and cover. Cook until the clams open, about 3 minutes. Remove the clams and their shells and set them aside. Turn the heat up and boil the clam sauce until it is reduced to approximately ½ cup. Strain and reserve.

6. Lightly coat a nonstick ovenproof sauté pan with olive oil. Season the fish fillets with sea salt, pepper, and thyme. Heat the pan until hot but not smoking. Place the fish skin side down in the pan and place the pan in the oven for approximately 7 minutes.

7. While the fish is in the oven, add the parsnips to the chanterelles and reheat. Just before serving, stir in the arugula and sauté for 10 seconds until just wilted.

8. Bring the clam sauce to a boil and whisk in the remaining butter. Turn down the heat and add the clams and their shells to gently reheat. This should take no more than 30 seconds.

9. Remove the fish from the oven. Place a pile of vegetables in the center of each plate or into the middle of a serving dish. Place the fillets on top of the vegetables. Surround the fish with the sauce and clams. Top with chopped chives.

Grilled Chicken with Garlic Mashed Potatoes & a Stir-Fry of Spring Vegetables

SERVES 4

Garlic Mashed Potatoes

2 pounds Yellow Finn, Yukon Gold, or any yellow-fleshed local potatoes, peeled and cut in large cubes

10 to 12 garlic cloves, peeled

½ cup heavy cream

6 to 8 ounces butter, cut in dices

Salt and pepper to taste

Place the potatoes and garlic cloves in a large saucepan. Cover with cold water, add a pinch of salt, and boil until the potatoes are soft. Drain the liquid, add heavy cream, and mash until most of the lumps are out. Work in the butter a little at a time, and season to taste with salt and pepper. Add more butter if you want richer, silkier mashed potatoes.

For the chicken:

2½ pounds free-range chicken, whole or parts (2 breasts, 2 legs with thighs attached, 2 wings)

3 tablespoons extra virgin olive oil

3 garlic cloves, peeled and coarsely chopped

2 tablespoons fresh basil leaves, coarsely chopped

2 tablespoons fresh thyme, coarsely chopped

Garlic Mashed Potatoes (see sidebar)

Stir-Fried Spring Vegetables (see sidebar on next page)

The day before grilling:

1. If the chicken is whole, cut into 6 parts so that you have 2 breasts, 2 legs with thighs attached, and 2 wings.

2. Mix together the olive oil, garlic, basil, and thyme. Toss the chicken parts in the mixture and allow to marinate overnight in the refrigerator.

The day of cooking:

3. Remove the chicken from the refrigerator 45 minutes before cooking. The chicken can be either broiled or grilled outside on a gas or charcoal barbecue. Be sure to prepare the grill or preheat your broiler 30 minutes before you start to cook.

4. Grill or broil the chicken for 30 minutes, turning and basting with olive oil every 5 minutes. Cover cooked chicken with foil to keep warm.

5. Make the garlic mashed potatoes.

6. Prepare the stir-fried vegetables.

7. To serve, make a mound of the potatoes in the middle of the plate. Top with a piece of chicken and spoon the vegetables over one edge of the chicken, letting them cascade to the bottom of the plate.

THE FORRESTAL
AT PRINCETON
HOTEL & CONFERENCE CENTER

The Forrestal
Princeton, New Jersey
Yves Vacheresse
Executive Chef

Stir-Fried Spring Vegetables*

1 tablespoon pure olive oil

½ bunch asparagus, cut on the diagonal into thin slices

½ pound spring spinach, cleaned, with stems removed

4 baby bok choy, cleaned and cut in thin strips

Salt and pepper to taste

For stir-fried vegetables, heat the olive oil in a nonstick pan until it is very hot but not smoking. Sauté the asparagus for a few minutes. Add the bok choy and cook for a few more minutes; then stir in the spinach. When the spinach has just wilted, season to taste with salt and pepper. For best results, make sure that the vegetables are sautéed quickly at very high temperature.

* You can use any fresh vegetables that are in season if you cannot find the ones used in this recipe.

"I landed at JFK International Airport in September 1977, a new immigrant arriving from France. Having crossed the Atlantic in the comfort of an Air France Boeing 747, my arrival to the New World was not as dramatic as it had been for other generations of immigrants. Like those before me, however, it was a powerful moment. With excitement, wonder, and a little fear coursing through you, at once you become aware that a new life is about to begin in a land that is very different than the one of your birth—the one you left behind.

I looked at everything. On the ride to Elizabeth, my first American home, my eyes scanned every detail of my new surroundings: the Verrazano-Narrows Bridge, the Manhattan skyline, the Statue of Liberty, the buildings, the road signs, the cars and trucks, the yellowish-beige-colored license plates bearing the caption New Jersey–The Garden State. I noticed the license plates on cars and trucks from other states and how each bore a summary of its home state's characteristics. But that could not hold true for New Jersey, I thought. There were no gardens to see anywhere in Elizabeth, Newark, Hackensack, Hasbrouck Heights, Fort Lee, or the other towns that compose the New York metropolitan area, which was all I knew of the Garden State. I wondered if the Meadowlands were what New Jerseyans referred to as their garden.

It was 10 years before I discovered that New Jersey was indeed a garden state. Here there are real farmers who produce a bounty of vegetables and fruits. Yet it was not until I connected and worked with the local organic growers and cooked and ate their fabulous products that the word garden truly came to life. It is an honor to feature a few recipes using the produce of these great local men and women, without whom my job would not be quite the same. "

Yves Vacheresse

Chilled Fennel & Leek Soup with Roasted Almond Pesto

SERVES 8

Roasted Almond Pesto

2 cups fresh basil leaves, washed and dried

⅓ cup slivered almonds, toasted

2 tablespoons Parmesan cheese, grated

2 cloves garlic, peeled

½ teaspoon kosher salt

¾ cup pure olive oil

Combine the basil, almonds, Parmesan cheese, garlic, and salt in a food processor. Process until all ingredients are finely ground. With the motor running, add the olive oil in a thin stream and process until the mixture thickens. Place the pesto in a medium bowl and chill.

For the soup:

2 tablespoons olive oil

2 large leeks, white parts only, sliced

2 cloves garlic, peeled and minced

1½ teaspoon fennel seeds

4 cups chicken stock

2 fennel bulbs, chopped

2 tablespoons fresh lemon juice

Salt and pepper

Roasted Almond Pesto (see sidebar)

1. Heat the olive oil in a 3-quart soup pan over medium heat. Add leeks and sauté until translucent. Add the garlic, chopped fennel, and fennel seeds and sauté for 5 more minutes.

2. Add the chicken stock and bring the mixture to a boil. Reduce the heat, cover, and simmer until the fennel is tender, about 30 minutes.

3. Puree the soup in batches in the food processor and transfer to a large bowl. Season the soup with lemon juice, salt, and pepper and chill for at least 3 hours.

4. To serve, ladle the soup into individual bowls and top each serving with 1 teaspoon of pesto.

The Bernards Inn
Bernardsville, New Jersey
Edward Stone
Executive Chef

Veal Chop with Morels, Porcini & Fava Beans

SERVES 4

3 tablespoons extra virgin olive oil

Unsalted butter

¼ pound fresh morels, split and brushed clean

¼ pound fresh porcini mushrooms, trimmed and sliced ¼-inch thick (If fresh porcini are not available, use any fresh fleshy mushroom such as portobello, crimini, or shiitake.)

Kosher salt

Pepper

2 to 3 pounds fresh fava beans

4 veal chops

1 tablespoon fresh thyme or savory, minced

1. Prepare a grill or preheat your broiler.

2. Heat 1 tablespoon of olive oil and 2 teaspoons of butter together in a sauté pan. When the butter has melted and the pan is hot, add the morels and porcini and sauté for 2 to 3 minutes. Sprinkle with kosher salt and pepper and continue cooking for another 2 minutes until the mushrooms are soft. Reserve.

3. Shuck the fava beans and blanch for 1 minute in boiling water or until the skins begin to loosen. Plunge the beans into ice water to cool. Pinch the casings to extract fava beans. (This is good work for your guests to do if they want to be in the kitchen with you.)

4. Season the veal chops with kosher salt and pepper. Grill or broil to your liking.

5. Rewarm the mushrooms and the favas in a tablespoon of butter or olive oil. Stir in the fresh thyme or savory and season with kosher salt and pepper to taste.

6. Place each veal chop on a plate and spoon the mushroom-and-fava-bean mixture generously around. Pour any juices from the meat over the top and serve.

ACROSS THE STREET

444 EAST 91 STREET

Across the Street
New York
Seen Lippert
Executive Chef

Risotto with Chicken Livers, Moscato d'Asti & Mushrooms

Chicken livers and sparkling Moscato d'Asti may never become as famous a gastronomic pairing as foie gras and Sauternes, but to our taste and for a lot less money, the combination works extremely well. The success of this risotto recipe does not depend on the wine's bubbles, so feel free to use Moscato from an opened bottle you may have enjoyed for a previous dessert, or find a bottle of any good California or French wine made from muscat grape.

Union Square Cafe
New York
Michael Romano
Executive Chef/Partner

SERVES 4 TO 6

5 to 6 cups chicken stock

1 pound chicken livers, trimmed

1 teaspoon kosher salt

¼ teaspoon freshly ground black pepper

3 tablespoons olive oil

2 tablespoons minced shallots

1 teaspoon minced garlic

¼ pound shiitake mushrooms, stemmed and sliced (2 cups)

1½ cups peeled and sliced carrots

1¾ cups Arborio rice

1½ cups Moscato wine

¾ cup snow peas, stemmed and cut into thirds

2 tablespoons butter

½ cup freshly grated Parmigiano-Reggiano

1. Bring the chicken stock to a simmer.

2. Season the chicken livers with ½ teaspoon salt and freshly grated black pepper. In a 3-quart heavy-bottomed skillet heat the olive oil over high flame and sear the livers, browning both sides, about 3 to 4 minutes. While they are still rare, remove the livers from the pan with a slotted spoon and reserve.

3. Add shallots and garlic to the pan and cook over a medium flame for 1 to 2 minutes, stirring to prevent browning. Stir in the shiitakes and carrots and cook 3 minutes. Add the rice and stir with a wooden spoon until coated with oil.

4. Reserve 2 tablespoons of the Moscato and add the remainder to the pan. Stir constantly over medium heat until the wine has been absorbed by the rice.

5. Ladle ½ cup of hot chicken stock into the pan and stir until it is absorbed. Continue with the rest of the stock, adding ½ cup at a time and letting each addition be absorbed completely into the rice before adding more liquid, resulting in the characteristic risotto creaminess.

The grains of rice should be al dente. Count on approximately 20 to 25 minutes for the rice to cook.

6. When all the stock has been used, stir in the snow peas and chicken livers, and heat through. Swirl in the butter, the reserved moscato, half the Parmigiano, the salt, and the pepper. Spoon the risotto into a warm serving bowl, sprinkle with the remaining cheese, and serve immediately.

Recipe taken from *The Union Square Cafe Cookbook*, published by HarperCollins, New York, 1994.

Grilled Asparagus with a Tomato & Lemon Thyme Emulsion

Lemon Thyme Oil

1 bunch lemon thyme

¾ cup extra virgin olive oil

Place lemon thyme and olive oil in a blender. Blend until the lemon thyme is roughly chopped. Place the lemon thyme–olive oil mixture into a covered plastic container—making sure that the thyme is completely immersed in the olive oil. Allow the mixture to sit, unrefrigerated, for 3 days. Strain and discard the lemon thyme. Reserve the oil.

SERVES 4

2 cups of New Jersey tomatoes, pureed and strained

Lemon Thyme Oil (see sidebar)

2 pounds of spring asparagus

Sea salt and freshly ground pepper to taste

1. To make the tomato-and-lemon-thyme emulsion, place the strained tomato juice into a saucepan and bring it to a boil. Boil the juice until it has reduced to ¼ cup and has a syrupy consistency.

2. Place the tomato syrup in a blender. With the motor running, add ½ cup lemon thyme oil in a slow stream until the sauce has emulsified and starts to thicken.

3. To prepare the asparagus, trim off the tough ends. Toss the asparagus with a few drops of lemon thyme oil and season with salt and pepper.

4. Grill the asparagus over a low flame until al dente. To serve, drizzle the asparagus with the tomato-and-lemon-thyme emulsion. Serve as a vegetable or add any kind of fresh tomato and serve as a salad.

Church Street Bistro
Lambertville, New Jersey
David G. Kiser
Chef/Proprietor

Asparagus with Braised Morels

SERVES 4 TO 6

For the morels:

5 tablespoons unsalted butter

1 medium shallot, peeled and chopped fine

1 large clove garlic, peeled and minced

½ teaspoon fresh thyme leaves, chopped

½ pound fresh morels, cleaned and cut into large pieces

½ cup dry white wine

½ cup chicken stock

Salt and freshly ground pepper

For the asparagus:

1½ pounds fresh asparagus

Sprigs of fresh thyme

1. Melt 4 tablespoons of butter in a large sauté pan over high heat. When the foam subsides and before the butter browns, stir in the shallots and garlic, sauté for 30 seconds, and then sprinkle in the thyme. Add the morels and cook until they are very lightly browned, 5 to 8 minutes. Add the wine and turn down the heat; simmer until the wine has almost evaporated. Gently stir in the stock and simmer until the liquid has reduced and thickened slightly. Season with salt and pepper and swirl in the remaining 1 tablespoon of butter.

2. Trim off the tough ends of the asparagus stalks so that they are a uniform 6 inches long. If the stalks are thick, trim them to a uniform length and peel the bottom half of each stalk with a vegetable peeler.

3. Bring ½ inch of water to a boil in a large frying pan that has a tight-fitting lid. Lay the asparagus in the boiling water, cover the pan, and boil vigorously just until the bottom end of a stalk can be pierced easily with the point of a sharp knife, 4 or 5 minutes. Drain the asparagus on paper towels, divide it among 6 plates, and spoon the morels across the middle of the asparagus, making sure that each serving includes a spoonful or 2 of the pan juices. Garnish each plate with a sprig of fresh thyme and serve immediately.

The Rainbow Room
New York
Waldy Malouf
Chef/Director

Mushrooms with Gremolata

Although this recipe was originally created to use fresh porcini mushrooms, it works well with any fresh fleshy mushroom such as portobello, crimini, shiitake, or even white button mushrooms.

SERVES 4

3 tablespoons olive oil

½ pound fresh mushrooms, cleaned and sliced ¼-inch thick

1 tablespoon unsalted butter

½ teaspoon kosher salt

¼ teaspoon pepper

2 cloves garlic, peeled and finely minced

Juice of 1 lemon

½ cup Italian parsley, chopped

Zest of ½ lemon, minced fine

1. Heat a sauté pan over medium-high flame. Add olive oil and let it warm for 30 seconds.

2. Add mushrooms and butter. Saute for 2 to 3 minutes or until golden brown and tender.

3. Season with kosher salt and pepper. Add minced garlic and cook for 1 minute more.

4. Spoon onto a serving plate, squeeze with fresh lemon juice, and sprinkle the parsley and lemon zest all over.

"*B*orn and raised in California's fertile Central Valley, I grew up eating fresh tomatoes, figs, and plums right from my own backyard. The connection to the land and all it provides for us was always apparent and appreciated.

This connection was strengthened further while working at Chez Panisse in Berkeley, California. The search for fresh and pure ingredients grown in ways that are ecologically sound is constant. I've extended these ideas to Across the Street restaurant here in Manhattan.

The Vinegar Factory market, where I shop for Across the Street, supports local and national organic farms and growers. The farmers supply us with fabulous products for the restaurant while taking care of the land for future generations. Across the Street, in return, creates seasonal menus that we hope will inspire our customers to allow local agriculture and the seasons to determine the choices they make at the market. *"*

Seen Lippert

ACROSS THE STREET

444 EAST 91 STREET

Across the Street
New York
Seen Lippert
Executive Chef

summer

Summer in the Northeast always means corn and tomatoes. Cucumber and peppers of all varieties are ready and there's always more than enough zucchini and eggplant. Those famous Jersey peaches as well as melons and berries are delicious when picked and eaten at their peak. Farm stands abound and U-pick farms are bursting with delicious summer fruits and vegetables from July to mid-September.

refreshing summer treats...

Create beautiful fruit salads with melons and berries and top with honey yogurt topping.

Blanch several ears of corn, cut the kernels from the cob, and mix with orzo, lemon zest, lemon juice, cold-pressed olive oil, and sea salt for a delicious orzo salad. Use the stripped cobs to create a tasty vegetable stock.

Make a quick gazpacho by placing coarsely chopped ripe tomatoes, cucumbers, onions, and green peppers in a blender. Blend until soupy but still chunky and season with olive oil, oregano, salt, pepper, and red wine vinegar. To be authentic, add some stale bread to the blender.

Grill a variety of vegetables, lightly marinated in your favorite vinaigrette, and enjoy hot or cold.

In separate pans, oven-roast salted, cubed, and lightly oiled eggplant, onions, zucchini, red and green peppers, and quartered Roma tomatoes. Combine with fresh herbs for a flavorful, updated version of ratatouille.

For a tasty oil-free salsa salad, toss cooked, cooled brown rice, chopped tomatoes, cilantro, scallions, jalapeño peppers, and lime juice with a pinch of salt.

Dress steamed string beans with a little coarse Dijon mustard and serve cold as a salad or hot as a side vegetable.

Create a salad of baby lettuces or Mesclun greens topped with a slice of Montrachet goat cheese, diced yellow pepper, peeled pear quarters roasted with thyme, and toasted walnuts. Dress it with a favorite vinaigrette.

Edibles...Naturally!
Princeton Junction
New Jersey
Alice Miller
Chef/Owner

Desert Garden Gazpacho with Margarita-Scallop Seviche

Margarita-Scallop Seviche

Seviche is a Latin American dish that uses lime juice instead of heat to "cook" raw seafood. The acid in the citrus juices slowly changes the proteins in the scallops rendering them "cooked" after a few hours. The tequila used in the marinade is just for flavor. If you prefer not to use it, leave it out.

2 limes, juice & minced zest

1 orange, juice & minced zest

3 tablespoons gold tequila

½ jalapeño pepper, seeded and minced

1 tablespoon chopped cilantro

2 scallions, thinly sliced

½ teaspoon salt

6 ounces sea scallops, sliced into ¼-inch coins

Combine all ingredients in a small bowl. Cover and refrigerate for at least 4 hours and no longer than 6 hours. Serve well chilled.

White Dog Cafe
Philadelphia
Kevin von Klause
Chef/Partner

1 green bell pepper, diced

1 cup fresh corn kernels

1 cucumber, peeled, seeded, and diced

1 cup diced peeled jicama

½ small red onion, peeled and diced

2 pounds ripe tomatoes, seeded and diced (about 4 cups)

1 teaspoon minced garlic

2 jalapeño peppers, seeded and minced

4 cups tomato juice

Juice of 1½ limes

¾ cup fresh orange juice

2 tablespoons chopped cilantro

1½ teaspoons salt

Margarita-Scallop Seviche (see sidebar)

1. Combine the bell pepper, corn, cucumber, jicama, onion, tomatoes, garlic, and jalapeños in a nonreactive large mixing bowl. Stir in tomato juice, lime juice, orange juice, cilantro, and salt. Chill well before serving. This soup is best if eaten within 2 days.

2. Serve in well-chilled bowls topped with ¼ cup of margarita-scallop seviche.

If you're hot and tired there are few things more energizing than a bowl of icy gazpacho. When the heat is on, whip up a batch of this cool crunchy soup and you won't mind it for long. We top it with a refreshing seviche of scallops marinated in golden tequila and zesty citrus juices. If you're in a hurry, the soup can be made by pureeing all of the vegetables in a food processor or blender. However, the texture is much nicer if you take the time to cut them by hand.

Recipe taken from *The White Dog Cafe Cookbook*, published by Running Press, Philadelphia, in press.

Tomato Confit

Make this when sweet 100s or other great cherry tomatoes are here in midsummer. This makes a terrific first course when served over grilled bread rubbed with garlic, or, as a main course, it is delicious over grilled fish with fresh arugula.

SERVES 4

1 pint cherry tomatoes

Salt and pepper

2 cloves garlic, peeled and thinly sliced

2 tablespoons balsamic vinegar

Extra virgin olive oil

1. Preheat oven to 350°F.

2. Place tomatoes in a single layer in a small ceramic baking dish. They can be fairly snug.

3. Sprinkle tomatoes with salt, pepper, and garlic.

4. Pour on the balsamic vinegar and enough extra virgin olive oil to come one-third the way up the sides of the tomatoes. This is a fairly extravagant use of olive oil, but it can be reused.

5. Place the tomatoes uncovered in the oven and bake for 1 hour or until tomatoes are slightly browned and very soft.

ACROSS THE STREET

444 EAST 91 STREET

Across the Street
New York
Seen Lippert
Executive Chef

Lemon-&-Herb Marinated Goat Cheese with Fresh Tomatoes

SERVES 4

We know how lucky we are to have farm-fresh produce delivered right to our door year round, but we are especially grateful in mid-July, when the bounty of sun-ripened tomatoes is not to be believed. Our favorites are some recently rediscovered heirloom varieties that are sweet and juicy with that real tomato flavor we remember from summers long past. This simple salad of marinated cheese is best made when the tomatoes are ripened by the sun and bursting with juice.

½ cup extra virgin olive oil

1 tablespoon chopped parsley leaves

1 tablespoon chopped basil leaves

¼ teaspoon freshly ground black pepper

¼ teaspoon salt

Pinch of hot red pepper flakes

1 lemon, thinly sliced into rounds

8 ounces fresh chèvre

4 ripe tomatoes, sliced

1. Whisk together the oil, parsley, basil, pepper, salt, and hot pepper flakes. Stir in the lemon rounds.

2. Divide the chèvre into 4 equal parts: shape each portion into a small disk. Arrange them in a single layer in a small bowl; pour on the lemon-and-oil marinade. Cover and set aside at room temperature for 6 hours turning once. (If you're not going to use the cheese right away, it can be refrigerated for up to 1 week. Bring to room temperature before serving, because the oil will solidify when chilled.)

3. Arrange the tomatoes on 4 chilled salad plates. Top with a disk of cheese and spoon some of the marinade over the top. Sprinkle with additional freshly ground black pepper and serve.

Other Ways to Do It: When tomatoes aren't in season, substitute spears of crisp romaine and rings of red and yellow bell peppers.

Recipe taken from *The White Dog Cafe Cookbook*, published by Running Press, Philadelphia, in press.

White Dog Cafe
Philadelphia
Kevin von Klause
Chef/Partner

Chinois Chicken Salad

Sweet & Spicy Vinaigrette

2 tablespoons Thai fish sauce

½ cup rice wine vinegar

1 tablespoon sugar

½ jalapeño, without seeds

¼ cup cilantro leaves

1 tablespoon ginger, finely minced

½ cup sesame oil

2 scallions

Salt and pepper

Place all of the ingredients, except the scallions, into a food processor or blender and blend for 2 minutes. Pour into a bowl and add scallions and salt and pepper to taste.

For the chicken:

3-pound roasting chicken, whole

1 tablespoon sesame oil

Salt and pepper

1 medium lemon, cut in quarters

1 medium red onion, peeled and cut in quarters

1 bunch cilantro, stems only; retain leaves for vinaigrette

For the noodles and vegetables:

1 pound rice noodles, cooked using instructions on package

¼ pound snow peas, julienned

2 ribs celery, cross sliced

1 medium cucumber, sliced

1 large red pepper, julienned

½ head napa cabbage, julienned

1 bunch scallions, sliced on the diagonal into rounds

1 large carrot, peeled and julienned

¼ cup roasted Spanish peanuts, chopped

Sweet & Spicy Vinaigrette (see sidebar)

1. Preheat oven to 450°F.
2. Rub the outside of the chicken with sesame oil. Season the cavity with salt and pepper, and stuff with lemon, onion, and cilantro stems. Place the chicken on rack in roasting pan. Brown at 450°F for 15 to 20 minutes. Turn the heat down to 350°F, season with salt and pepper, and roast for 30 to 40 minutes. Check for doneness. Remove from oven and cool to room temperature.
3. When the chicken has cooled, remove the skin and "pull" the meat into long thin strips. Julienne the leg meat into 1-x-⅛-inch pieces. Remove the lemons from the cavity and squeeze over the chicken. Season with salt and pepper.
4. Cook the noodles and cool. Toss the noodles with a few tablespoons of vinaigrette. Divide into 4 to 6 equal portions and place around the outside edge of each plate.
5. Toss the vegetables with half of the vinaigrette. Place a pile of vegetables in the center of each plate, top with chicken, and finish with the remaining vegetables. Garnish with chopped peanuts and cilantro leaves.

Arthur's Landing Restaurant
Weehawken, New Jersey
Steven Singer
Executive Chef

June Harvest Bluefish Roast

Lemon-Mint Vinaigrette

⅓ cup fresh lemon juice

1 small shallot, peeled

2 garlic cloves, peeled

1 teaspoon peppercorns

1 cup fresh spearmint or wild mint, coarsely chopped

¼ cup cider vinegar

2 teaspoons kosher salt

1½ cups extra virgin olive oil

In a food processor or blender, combine the lemon juice, shallot, garlic, peppercorns, mint, vinegar, and salt. Process until completely pureed.

With the motor running, add the olive oil in a slow stream until emulsified.

Use this summer flavor combination for either marinating, basting, or just drizzling over bluefish, tuna, swordfish, grilled chicken or turkey, or chilled squid or shrimp or as a great dressing for new potatoes and string beans.

New World Cafe
Woodstock, New York
Ric Orlando
Executive Chef/Partner

SERVES 6

24 to 36 pearl onions, blanched and peeled (see step 2)

4 cups long-grain brown rice

6 six-ounce fresh skinless bluefish fillets

1 cup **Lemon-Mint Vinaigrette** (see sidebar)

1 pound sugar snap peas

1 pound baby cherry tomatoes; use mix of red and yellow

Mint sprigs for garnish

1. Preheat oven to 450°F.

2. To prepare the pearl onions, bring a 2-quart pot of water to a boil. Prepare a bowl of ice water and set it next to the stove. Cut off the root and stem ends of the onions. Be careful that the layers of onion remain attached when removing the root end. Drop the onions into boiling water for 1 minute and then immediately into the ice water. When cool, drain the onions and gently squeeze them out of their skins. Return the peeled onions to the boiling water and blanch for 3 minutes. Drain and reserve.

3. To prepare the rice, combine the brown rice with 8 cups of water and a teaspoon of salt. Bring to a boil and then turn the heat down as low as possible. Cover and simmer the rice on low heat for 20 to 25 minutes.

4. Arrange bluefish fillets in a large ovenproof skillet. Make sure the fillets are not touching each other. Rub each fillet with a tablespoon of the vinaigrette. Roast at 450°F for 10 to 12 minutes or until cooked but still moist.

5. Remove the fish from the pan and cover with foil to keep warm. In the same pan, combine the onions, snap peas, cherry tomatoes, and ½ cup of the vinaigrette. Sauté for 30 seconds. Then turn off the heat and reserve.

6. To serve, arrange rice on each plate. Lean one fillet onto each bed of rice, and spoon the vegetables over the top. Add 1 to 2 tablespoons of vinaigrette over each fillet and garnish with lots of mint sprigs.

On the Connecticut coast, bluefish is the fish of choice in summer. When it is fresh, it is sublime. The lemony dressing and sweet local veggies balance the rich oiliness of the fish perfectly.

Tangy Summer Vegetable Tian

A zesty tian of garden-fresh vegetables and herbs, this dish makes use of late summer's surplus of tomatoes, basil, and zucchini. It is best served at room temperature, making it a natural supper for sultry nights. We squeeze as many vegetables as possible into the tian, so it must be pressed when it comes out of the oven to make it more compact and easy to serve.

SERVES 4 TO 8

½ cup chopped basil

2 tablespoons chopped oregano

1 tablespoon chopped thyme leaves

6 tablespoons extra virgin olive oil

6 tablespoons red wine vinegar

1 eggplant, sliced into ¼-inch rings

½ cup grated Parmesan cheese

2 tablespoons minced garlic

Salt and freshly ground black pepper

3 tomatoes cut into ¼-inch slices

1 zucchini cut on a diagonal into ¼-inch slices

2 portobello mushrooms, cut into ¼-inch slices

1 red onion, peeled and sliced into thin rings

1 yellow squash cut on a diagonal into ¼-inch slices

1. Preheat the oven to 400°F.

2. Combine the basil, oregano, and thyme in a small bowl. In a separate bowl, whisk together the olive oil and vinegar.

3. Arrange a single layer of the eggplant slices in the bottom of a 10-x-6-inch baking pan. Sprinkle with a few tablespoons of the vinaigrette, some of the mixed herbs, a sprinkling of cheese, a pinch of minced garlic, a pinch of salt, and a grinding of black pepper. Top with a layer of sliced tomatoes. Top the tomatoes with more of the vinaigrette, herbs, cheese, garlic, salt, and pepper. Repeat with the zucchini, mushrooms, onion, yellow onion, yellow squash, and remaining eggplant. Make sure that each layer including the final one is topped with some of the vinaigrette, herbs, cheese, garlic, salt, and pepper. When finished, the layered vegetables will probably be higher than the sides of the pan.

4. Oil a piece of aluminum foil and cover the vegetables tightly. Set on the middle rack of the oven with a baking sheet underneath to catch any juices. Bake for 1 hour and 15 minutes. Remove from the oven, uncover, and carefully pour off all of the excess juices into a bowl. Reserve the liquid.

5. Place the tian on a baking sheet and re-cover it with the

White Dog Cafe
Philadelphia
Kevin von Klause
Chef/Partner

foil. Place another baking pan of the same size on top of it and lay something heavy (ideally a brick, but cans of soup will work) on top to weigh it down. When the weight is placed on, some of the juices may spill over the sides, so be sure the tian is on a baking sheet to catch any spills. Let set at room temperature for 1 hour. Remove the weights and foil. Pour any remaining liquid off and add to the reserved juices.

6. Pour the reserved juices into a saucepan and bring to a boil over high heat. Cook until reduced to a thick, syrupy consistency, about 5 minutes.

7. Cut the tian into wedges and serve at room temperature. Drizzle each piece with some of the reduced vegetable juices. The tian will keep refrigerated for 2 days. Bring to room temperature before serving.

Recipe taken from *The White Dog Cafe Cookbook*, published by Running Press, Philadelphia, in press.

"*W*hen I first started cooking in Philadelphia, I was introduced to Mark and Judy Dornstreich of Branch Creek Farm, in Perkasie, Pennsylvania, who grew some of the most gorgeous organic produce I had ever seen. The days when Mark or Judy delivered their harvest were looked upon with great anticipation. All the busy cooks stopped to admire and sample what they'd brought: painstakingly nurtured baby squash with blossoms still attached, a galaxy of edible flowers, bouquets of freshly cut herbs, miniature head lettuces, tiny pear tomatoes, and unique heirloom varieties of peppers and eggplants. Their stunning produce turned me on to using organic fruits and vegetables.

Today we purchase produce from other local farms and cooperatives as well. They produce the ingredients needed to make the delicious, wholesome food our customers have come to love and expect. Without question, those farms are the secret behind our success. We choose to use these ingredients not only to ensure a great meal but also to support the organic farmers in our region. Doing this is good for our bodies, the local economy, the land around us, and the planet at large. Through the White Dog Cafe kitchen, I try to excite people about the promise and pleasure of cooking with organic ingredients by serving fabulous food that is raised in a sane manner, by people I know. *"*

Kevin von Klause

Double Corn & Blueberry Pancakes with Maple-Pine Nut Butter

Maple-Pine Nut Butter

½ pound unsalted butter, at room temperature

½ cup pure maple syrup

¼ cup plus 2 tablespoons pine nuts, toasted

Place the butter in a food processor and process for 30 seconds to whip. With the motor running, slowly pour in the syrup and process for 15 seconds. Scrape down the sides with a rubber spatula and process for 10 seconds.

Remove the butter to a small bowl and fold in the pine nuts. Serve immediately or place the whipped butter on a piece of plastic wrap or parchment paper and roll it into a cylinder 2 inches in diameter. Refrigerate until firm and then slice into medallions before serving. The roll of butter can be frozen for up to 2 months.

4 tablespoons unsalted butter

1 cup fresh or frozen sweet corn kernels (fresh is best)

¾ cup all-purpose flour

¼ cup cornmeal

3 tablespoons sugar

¼ teaspoon salt

1½ teaspoons baking powder

¾ teaspoon baking soda

¼ teaspoon ground allspice

1 large egg

½ cup buttermilk

½ cup whole milk

1 cup fresh blueberries

Maple-Pine Nut Butter (see sidebar)

1. Melt butter in a sauté pan set over medium-high heat. Add the corn and sauté for 1 minute; reserve.

2. Sift the flour, cornmeal, sugar, salt, baking powder, baking soda, and allspice in a large bowl. Whisk together the egg, buttermilk, milk, and sautéed corn.

3. Add the wet ingredients to the dry ingredients and mix until just combined; it is all right if there are a few lumps. Fold in the blueberries.

4. Heat a griddle over medium-high heat until a drop of water sprinkled on it sizzles. Pour scant ½-cupfuls of the batter onto the griddle and cook until the bubbles that form around the outside edges pop: 2 to 3 minutes. Flip the pancakes and cook the other side until golden brown. Repeat with the remaining batter. Serve with maple-pine nut butter.

Recipe taken from *The White Dog Cafe Cookbook*, published by Running Press, Philadelphia, in press.

We make these pancakes when the New Jersey corn is high and the blueberries are plump and juicy—from mid-July through August. You can make them with frozen corn kernels and frozen blueberries, but some of the sweetness is lost, so add a bit more sugar.

White Dog Cafe
Philadelphia
Kevin von Klause
Chef/Partner

Ragout of Fingerling Potatoes, Eggplant & Heirloom Tomatoes

SERVES 8

2 pounds fingerling potatoes, washed and cut on the diagonal
    into ½-inch-thick pieces

4 tablespoons pure olive oil

Salt and pepper to taste

3 medium Japanese eggplants, cut into ½-inch dice

2 red peppers, cut in thick strips

1 or 2 jalapeño peppers, seeds removed, finely chopped

1 large red onion, peeled and diced

4 garlic cloves, peeled and chopped

1 piece ginger (1 to 2 ounces), peeled and grated

½ teaspoon turmeric

2 large Heirloom tomatoes, diced

½ bunch fresh cilantro, stems removed, coarsely chopped

1. Preheat the oven to 450°F.

2. Heat 1 tablespoon of olive oil in a sauté pan large enough to hold all of the potatoes without crowding. Add the potatoes and sauté over medium-high heat until golden brown. Season with salt and pepper and reserve.

3. Toss the eggplant with 2 tablespoons olive oil and season with salt and pepper. Place the eggplant on a roasting pan and roast at 450°F until light brown and soft, about 15 to 20 minutes.

4. Heat 1 tablespoon of olive oil in a heavy-bottomed saucepan. Sauté the red peppers, jalapeño peppers, and onion over medium heat for 5 minutes or until soft. Add the garlic and ginger and sauté for a few more minutes. Stir in turmeric and cook for 2 minutes.

5. Add the tomatoes and cook for 5 minutes. Add the reserved potatoes and eggplants. Cook for 20 minutes on low heat. If the mixture seems dry, add water.

6. Garnish with chopped cilantro and serve.

The Forrestal
Princeton, New Jersey
Yves Vacheresse
Executive Chef

Risotto d'Oro

This golden-colored risotto looks convincingly like risotto alla milanese—the saffron-infused Lombardy classic. But appearance is where the similarity ends. Substituting fresh carrot and celery juices for the standard chicken stock adds a gentle sweetness to this summery, all-vegetable risotto. A vegetable juicer makes this recipe convenient to prepare, but fresh vegetable juices are widely available in health food stores.

SERVES 4 TO 6

3 cups carrot juice

3 cups celery juice

$1/4$ cup olive oil

$1^3/4$ cups Arborio rice

$1/2$ teaspoon minced garlic

$1/2$ cup white wine

$1/2$ cup peeled, split lengthwise, and sliced carrots

$1/2$ cup 1-inch pieces green beans

$1/2$ cup split lengthwise and sliced zucchini

$1/2$ cup $1/2$-inch pieces asparagus, tough ends discarded

$1/2$ cup sliced red bell pepper

$1/2$ cup fresh shelled peas

$1/3$ cup sliced scallions

4 tablespoons butter

$3/4$ cup finely grated Parmigiano-Reggiano

1 teaspoon kosher salt

$1/8$ teaspoon freshly ground black pepper

1 tablespoon chopped parsley

1. In a saucepan, combine the carrot and celery juices and bring to simmer.

2. In a 3-quart skillet, heat the olive oil over medium heat. Add the rice and garlic and stir together until rice is coated with oil. Add the white wine and bring to a boil, stirring constantly until the rice absorbs the wine. Add the carrots and the green beans to the rice.

3. Ladle $1/2$ cup of the hot juice mixture into the saucepan and stir until it is absorbed. Continue with the rest of the juice, adding $1/2$ cup at a time and letting each addition be absorbed completely into the rice before adding more liquid. The constant stirring allows the rice to release its starch into the cooking liquid, resulting in the characteristic risotto creaminess. When $3/4$ of the juice has been used, about 15 to 20 minutes, stir in the remaining

Union Square Cafe

Union Square Cafe
New York
Michael Romano
Executive Chef/Partner

vegetables and continue ladling and stirring in the remaining juice, about 10 minutes. The grains of rice should be al dente.

4. Swirl in the butter and ³/₄ of the Parmigiano, and season with salt and pepper. Serve the risotto sprinkled with parsley and the remaining Parmigiano.

Recipe taken from *The Union Square Cafe Cookbook*, published by HarperCollins, New York, 1994.

Tomato Salad with Truffle Vinaigrette

Mushroom Juice

1 pound white mushrooms, wiped and sliced

½ cup water

Place mushrooms and water in a saucepan. Bring to a boil, stirring occasionally. Cover and simmer for 30 minutes. Remove the pan from heat and strain the mushrooms through a fine mesh strainer, reserving the juice. Put the juice back into the pan and reduce to ¼ cup over high heat.

The Ryland Inn
Whitehouse, New Jersey
Craig Shelton
Executive Chef/Proprietor

SERVES 4

For the truffle vinaigrette:

¹/₃ cup sherry wine vinegar

¹/₃ cup balsamic vinegar

Splash of red wine vinegar

¹/₄ cup **Mushroom Juice** (see sidebar)

1 tablespoon white truffle oil

½ cup extra virgin olive oil

½ cup canola oil

Sea salt, to taste

White pepper, ground, to taste

For the salad:

2 large tomatoes, very ripe, sliced

2 shallots, peeled and finely chopped

4 tablespoons fresh chives, chopped

Baby lettuces

Herb mix (use sweet herbs such as chervil and chives)

1. To make the vinaigrette, combine the balsamic vinegar, sherry vinegar, and red wine vinegar and stir in the mushroom juice. Whisk in the white truffle oil, olive oil, and canola oil. Season with salt and pepper to taste.

2. Season tomatoes with salt, pepper, shallots, and chives. Arrange tomatoes on plate.

3. Dress lettuce with vinaigrette and place on top of tomatoes. Top with fresh herbs.

Chopped Organic Vegetable Salad

Frisco Green Goddess Dressing

MAKES 2 CUPS

2 egg yolks

2 tablespoons Dijon mustard

2 cloves garlic

¼ cup sour cream

1 cup olive oil

⅛ cup champagne vinegar

¼ cup lemon juice

¼ cup chives, minced

¼ cup tarragon, minced

¼ cup scallions, minced

Salt and pepper

Combine eggs, Dijon mustard, garlic, and sour cream in a food processor or blender.

Slowly drizzle in olive oil until emulsified.

Remove and transfer to a mixing bowl. Stir in vinegar, lemon juice, chives, tarragon, and green onions. Season with salt and pepper. Chill before serving.

Arthur's Landing Restaurant
Weehawken, New Jersey
Steven Singer, Executive Chef

SERVES 4

½ cup yellow wax beans, ¼-inch cuts, blanched and chilled

½ cup green beans, ¼-inch cuts, blanched and chilled

1 cup fava or garbanzo beans, cooked and chilled (optional)

1 large avocado, ½-inch dice

½ cucumber, peeled, seeded, ½-inch dice

½ cup radishes, ¼-inch dice

1 cup broccoli florets, separated into bite-size pieces

1 cup cauliflower florets, separated into bite-size pieces

12 red cherry tomatoes, cut in halves

12 yellow cherry tomatoes, cut in halves

1 bunch scallions, sliced thin, green part only

1 bunch arugula, julienned fine

1 head radicchio, julienned fine

1 head romaine hearts, julienned fine

1 lemon

Salt and pepper

1 cup **Frisco Green Goddess Dressing** (see sidebar)

1. To blanch the green and yellow beans, immerse them in a pot of boiling water to which a generous pinch of salt has been added. Boil for 2 minutes. Taste the beans to check for doneness. They should be tender but slightly crisp. Plunge the beans into a bowl of ice water. Cool and drain.

2. Shuck the fava beans and blanch for 1 minute. Pinch the casings to extract the beans. If using garbanzos, soak 1 cup dried beans overnight in cold water. Drain and cover by 3 inches with fresh water. Simmer 1 hour or until soft.

3. Combine the beans with the avocado, cucumber, radishes, cauliflower, cherry tomatoes, and scallions. Add 1 cup of Frisco green goddess dressing and toss.

4. Toss the arugula, radicchio, and romaine hearts with salt, pepper, and the juice of 1 lemon. Divide these greens equally onto four plates and top each pile of greens with a generous portion of vegetables. Serve.

Lavender Biscuits with Mixed Summer Berries

SERVES 6

Mixed Berries

2 generous pints ripe mixed berries such as blueberries, strawberries, raspberries, or blackberries

Place the berries in a large bowl and toss with the sugar. Use the back of a wooden spoon to crush some of the berries into the sugar. Let stand at room temperature for at least ½ hour or until the berries begin to exude some of their natural juices. Chill.

Mixed Berries (see sidebar)

⅓ cup sugar (or to taste)

2 cups all-purpose flour

1 teaspoon salt

2 tablespoons sugar

1 tablespoon baking powder

2 teaspoons lavender flowers (available in specialty stores)

4 ounces unsalted butter, cut into ¼-inch cubes

1 cup heavy cream plus extra for glaze

1 tablespoon sugar crystals (available in specialty stores)

2 cups crème fraîche, whipped, for serving

1. Preheat the oven to 350°F. Butter a baking sheet.

2. Prepare mixed berries.

3. Sift together the flour, salt, sugar, and baking powder in a large mixing bowl. Add lavender flowers. Using a pastry blender or your hand, cut in the butter until the dough resembles coarse meal. Add 1 cup of the heavy cream and mix just to form a rough dough; it will be quite tacky.

4. Flour a work surface. Using your fingertips, pat the dough out to an even ¾-inch thickness. Cut the dough into rounds with a 3-inch biscuit cutter. Transfer the biscuits to a buttered baking sheet. Gather the scraps of dough, pat out again, and cut out the remaining biscuits. Brush the tops lightly with the remaining heavy cream and sprinkle with sugar crystals. The biscuits can be made up to this point 24 hours in advance. Cover them with plastic wrap and refrigerate until ready to bake.

5. Bake for 18 to 20 minutes or until cooked through and just beginning to brown. Cool slightly and cut horizontally. Place the bottoms of the biscuits on serving plates. Spoon the berries generously over the biscuits, dividing them evenly and spooning the juice over. Spoon some of the crème fraîche over the berries and replace the biscuit lids. Serve immediately.

Recipe taken from *The White Dog Cafe Cookbook*, published by Running Press, Philadelphia, in press.

White Dog Cafe
Philadelphia
Kevin von Klause
Chef/Partner

Roasted Trout with Summer Vegetables

SERVES 4

For the vegetables:

10 tablespoons extra virgin olive oil

2 small Italian eggplants (about ¼ pound each), cut in 6 slices each

Salt and freshly ground pepper

1 medium zucchini, cut on the bias into 12 slices

1 medium yellow summer squash, cut on the bias into 12 slices

¾ cup shredded basil leaves

1 medium onion, peeled and cut in half and each half cut into 6 slices

1 large ripe tomato, cut in half and each half cut into 6 slices

For the trout:

4 whole 12-ounce trout, boned, with heads removed and fins trimmed

Juice of 1 lemon

Fresh basil leaves

Extra olive oil, if needed

1. Preheat the broiler. Lightly oil a 10-x-15-inch jelly roll pan with olive oil. Lay the eggplant slices on it, sprinkle them with salt and brush a little more olive oil over them. Broil the eggplant 5 minutes on each side and let cool. Turn the oven down to 450°F.

2. Combine the zucchini and yellow squash in a bowl and toss with ¼ cup olive oil, the shredded basil, and some salt and pepper.

3. On an oiled 10-x-15-inch jelly roll pan, arrange the sliced vegetables by placing the zucchini, summer squash, tomato, onion, and eggplant alternately in a shingle pattern. There should be 20 slices per row and 3 rows in all. Sprinkle over the vegetables any oil and basil remaining in the bowl.

4. Bake the vegetables for about 30 minutes, until they are tender and the pan juices have evaporated. Using a

The Rainbow Room
New York
Waldy Malouf
Chef/Director

spatula, lift the vegetables off the pan and arrange them decoratively around the edge of a large platter that will eventually hold the fish. The vegetables may be baked several hours in advance and served at room temperature.

5. If you have cooked the vegetables in advance, preheat the oven to 400°F. If you have cooked the vegetables immediately before cooking the fish, turn the oven down to 400°F.

6. Season the cavity of each trout with salt and about a tablespoon of shredded basil. Oil a baking pan with olive oil and lay the trout on it. Sprinkle the lemon juice and the remaining olive oil over the trout and roast for 10 minutes. Then turn on the broiler and broil the trout, without turning them over, for 5 minutes.

7. Carefully transfer the trout to the prepared platter. Pour the pan juices over the fish and decorate the platter with fresh basil leaves.

Fresh Tomato Soup

SERVES 4

3 ripe Jersey tomatoes, peeled, seeded, and chopped

1 bunch fresh basil, cleaned

1 bunch fresh mint, cleaned

Fine sea salt and freshly ground pepper to taste

Extra virgin olive oil

1. Place the chopped tomatoes in a food processor. Puree until completely smooth with absolutely no lumps. Strain the pureed tomatoes, pushing as much pulp as possible through the strainer.

2. Put the strained tomatoes back into the food processor and puree with the basil and mint. Season to taste with sea salt and pepper.

3. To serve, drizzle with olive oil and garnish with basil or mint.

Church Street Bistro
Lambertville, New Jersey
David G. Kiser
Chef/Proprietor

Jumbo Lump Crab Cakes with Stir-Fried Vegetables

Crab Cake Sauce

¼ cup butter

2 shallots, peeled and finely minced

½ cup white wine

5 tablespoons Dijon mustard

5 tablespoons whole-grain mustard

2 cups heavy cream

Salt and pepper

Melt 2 tablespoons of butter in a saucepan. Add shallots and cook until soft. Add white wine and boil until reduced to ¼ cup. Stir in the mustards and cream and bring back to a boil. Cook over medium heat until the sauce has thickened and will coat the back of a spoon. Whisk in the remaining 2 tablespoons of cold butter and season to taste with salt and pepper.

1 pound jumbo lump crabmeat

⅛ cup parsley, finely chopped

⅛ cup red onion, peeled and finely chopped

⅛ cup celery, finely chopped

1 tablespoon Old Bay seasoning

1 teaspoon salt

1 teaspoon white pepper

3 tablespoons Dijon mustard

1 tablespoon Tabasco sauce

2 tablespoons Worcestershire sauce

2 tablespoons fresh lemon juice

2 whole eggs, beaten

2½ cups bread crumbs

4 tablespoons vegetable oil

2 teaspoons unsalted butter

Crab Cake Sauce (see sidebar)

Vegetables for Crab Cakes (see sidebar on next page)

1. Pick the crabmeat, being careful to remove all shells and cartilage. Avoid breaking up the large pieces of crab. Toss crabmeat with parsley, onion, celery, Old Bay seasoning, salt, and pepper.

2. Mix together the Dijon mustard, Tabasco, Worcestershire, lemon juice, and eggs and combine with crabmeat.

3. To form the cakes, add bread crumbs to the crabmeat mixture in ¼-cup increments until the mixture holds together when shaped into a ball. Form 4 large or 6 medium crab cakes. Refrigerate the cakes while you prepare the vegetables and sauce. The cakes can be refrigerated for up to 24 hours.

4. Prepare the crab cake sauce and vegetables.

Arthur's Landing Restaurant
Weehawken, New Jersey
Steven Singer
Executive Chef

Vegetables for Crab Cakes

2 tablespoons canola oil

1 large red pepper, julienned

1 large carrot, peeled and julienned

1 medium red onion, peeled and sliced thin

1 large zucchini, julienned

1 large yellow squash, julienned

1 medium bok choy, sliced on a bias

2 cups snow peas, whole

½ head napa cabbage, julienned

1 bunch watercress

Heat the oil in a large sauté pan. Add the vegetables in the following order—red pepper, carrots, red onion, squashes, boy choy, napa cabbage, and watercress— and cook them quickly on high heat, stirring frequently. If you don't have a pan large enough to accommodate all of the vegetables, cook each one separately and then combine them.

Season with salt and pepper.

5. To cook the crabcakes, coat the outside of the cakes with the remaining bread crumbs. Choose a sauté pan that can hold all of the cakes without crowding. Heat the vegetable oil and butter together over medium-high heat until hot but not smoking. Gently place the crab cakes in the pan and cook for 4 minutes on each side.

6. To serve, place the sauce in a large pool on a heated plate. Mound equal portions of the vegetables in the center of each plate. Top with a hot, crispy, cooked crab cake.

To find out more about blue crabs, visit the Crabbing: All about Blue Crabs Web site at www.clark.net/pub/crabbing. This interesting site contains lots of information on catching and cooking crabs, including:

- *the life cycle of the blue crab*
- *descriptions of the various methods and tools used by commercial and sport crabbers to catch crabs*
- *crabbing laws in Delaware, Maryland, and Virginia*
- *a glossary of crabbing terms*
- *information on how to clean, cook, pick, and freeze hard- and soft-shell crabs*

Sautéed Chicken with Tarragon & Tomato Sauce

Peeling and Seeding Tomatoes

Prepare a large bowl of ice water and set aside. Using a sharp paring knife, remove tomato stems by cutting a cone shaped piece from the top of each tomato. Score the bottom of each tomato with a small X-shaped cut.

Bring a large pot of water to a boil. Drop 2 or 3 tomatoes into the boiling water and boil for 15 to 20 seconds. Using a slotted spoon, remove each tomato from the boiling water and plunge it into the ice bath. Once the tomato has cooled, take it out of the ice water and peel off the skin. You can do several tomatoes at once.

The Rainbow Room
New York
Waldy Malouf
Chef/Director

SERVES 4

For the chicken:

8 pieces of chicken, breast, thighs, or legs

Kosher salt and freshly ground pepper

Flour for dredging

¼ cup vegetable oil

For the sauce:

2 tablespoons unsalted butter

1 shallot, peeled and minced

1 clove garlic, peeled and minced

2 tablespoons chopped fresh tarragon leaves and stems

½ cup dry white wine

2 tablespoons white wine vinegar with tarragon

3 large ripe tomatoes, rough chopped

1 cup chicken stock

4 tablespoons unsalted butter, very cold, cut in small chunks

1 teaspoon chopped fresh tarragon

1 small tomato, peeled, seeded and diced

Tarragon sprigs

1. Preheat the oven to 375°F.

2. Wipe the chicken dry with paper towels and season it with salt and pepper. Dredge the chicken in flour, shaking off the excess.

3. In an ovenproof sauté pan, heat the oil; add the chicken, skin side down; and brown it over moderate heat for 7 to 8 minutes until it is crisp and golden.

4. Turn the chicken over and continue to cook for another 3 or 4 minutes. (If your sauté pan is not big enough to comfortably accommodate all the chicken, brown it in 2 batches.) Remove the chicken from the pan and set it aside.

5. Continue to cook the fat (being careful not to burn the solids) until the solids stick to the pan and the fat is clear. Discard the fat and let the pan cool for a few minutes.

6. Melt 2 tablespoons of butter in the pan. Add the shallot and garlic and cook, stirring, until they are lightly browned.

7. Add the chopped tarragon, wine, and vinegar, and bring to a simmer, stirring to incorporate all the browned bits.

8. Reduce the liquid by half and add the tomatoes and stock. Bring the liquid to a boil and return the chicken to the pan, skin side up.

9. Put the chicken in the oven and bake uncovered for 10 minutes. Then remove the breast pieces, keep them warm, and cook the dark meat 5 minutes longer.

10. Remove the chicken to a serving plate and keep it warm in the turned-off oven.

11. Pass the sauce through a food mill or press it through a strainer, leaving only the tomato skins and seeds behind.

12. Bring the sauce to a boil and reduce it until it begins to thicken and look shiny. You should have about 1½ cups. Turn the heat to low, season the sauce with salt and pepper, and whisk in the cold butter.

13. Pour the sauce over the chicken, sprinkle with chopped tarragon, and garnish with diced tomato and tarragon sprigs.

Sliced Tomatoes with Champagne

SERVES 4

2 pounds ripe tomatoes, sliced or quartered

1 shallot, peeled and minced fine

Fleur de sel or kosher salt

Champagne

ACROSS THE STREET

444 EAST 91 STREET

Across the Street
New York
Seen Lippert
Executive Chef

1. Arrange tomatoes on a plate. Sprinkle with salt and minced shallot.

2. Drizzle with chilled champagne and serve.

For this dish you must find the best vine-ripened tomatoes possible. Choose an assortment of varieties and colors from your local farmers market.

Grilled Corn with Cumin Butter

Some folks soak their corn in water before grilling it, but we like to place it straight on the grill. The smoldering outer husks give the sweet corn a fabulous smoky quality that is enhanced by the spicy lime-spiked cumin butter.

SERVES 8

½ pound unsalted butter, at room temperature

¼ cup finely minced red onion

1 teaspoon minced garlic

½ jalapeño pepper, seeded and minced

1 tablespoon ground cumin

⅓ whole lime, seeded and finely minced (about 2 teaspoons)

1 tablespoon finely chopped cilantro

¾ teaspoon salt

8 ears sweet corn

1. Melt 2 tablespoons of the butter in a small sauté pan set over medium heat. Add the onion and cook until translucent, about 4 minutes. Add the garlic and jalapeño and cook for 2 minutes. Stir in the cumin and cook for 1 minute. Remove from heat.

2. Combine the cumin mixture, remaining butter, lime, cilantro, and salt in a bowl and mix well with a fork until the butter is smooth and all of the ingredients are incorporated. There should be no lumps of butter in the mixture.

3. Spoon the butter onto a piece of waxed paper or plastic wrap. Shape into a log 2 inches in diameter. Roll up tightly and refrigerate until firm. The butter will keep refrigerated for up to 2 weeks.

4. Prepare the charcoal grill.

5. Place the ears of corn in their husks on the grill. Grill, turning frequently until all sides have started to char, about 8 to 10 minutes.

6. Pull back a large piece of husk from each ear of corn. Place a 1-ounce medallion of cumin butter on the exposed kernels of corn. Arrange the corn on a large platter and serve immediately.

Recipe taken from *The White Dog Cafe Cookbook*, published by Running Press, Philadelphia, in press.

White Dog Cafe
Philadelphia
Kevin von Klause
Chef/Partner

Grilled Shrimp, Conghilie Pasta & Heirloom Tomatoes

SERVES 6

For the shrimp:

36 to 48 medium shrimp, peeled and deveined

3 to 4 garlic cloves, peeled and chopped coarsely

1 tablespoon fresh rosemary, chopped

1 tablespoon fresh thyme, chopped

1 tablespoon fresh oregano, chopped

¼ cup extra virgin olive oil

For the pasta:

1½ pounds conghilie (shell-shaped) pasta

1 tablespoon olive oil

1 teaspoon finely chopped garlic

6 medium ripe heirloom tomatoes, cut in ¼-inch dice

½ bunch fresh basil leaves, cut into thin strips

¼ cup extra virgin olive oil

Kosher salt and pepper to taste

1. Marinate the shrimp for 1 to 2 hours in the garlic, rosemary, thyme, oregano, and olive oil.

2. The shrimp can be grilled or broiled. Prepare a grill or preheat the broiler 30 minutes before cooking. Scrape the marinade off the shrimp and season with salt and pepper. Grill or broil 2 to 3 inches from the heat source for 3 to 4 minutes on each side. Cover with foil to keep warm.

3. Bring a large pot of water to a boil. Add 1 tablespoon of kosher salt and the pasta. Cook until al dente so that the pasta still has some firmness but no crunch. Drain and reserve.

4. Heat 1 tablespoon olive oil in a sauté pan over medium-high heat. Sauté garlic for 30 seconds until light brown. Stir in the tomatoes and cooked pasta shells. Heat for 1 to 2 minutes.

5. Remove the pan from the fire and add the basil, shrimp, and extra virgin olive oil. When adding the oil, put half in first and then season with salt and pepper. Taste and add more oil if desired. Serve warm.

The Forrestal
Princeton, New Jersey
Yves Vacheresse
Executive Chef

Cream of Watercress Soup

SERVES 4

1 large bundle watercress, well rinsed

1 cup vegetable stock or chicken stock

1 tablespoon dry sherry

2 tablespoons cornstarch

1 teaspoon honey

1 cup milk or half-and-half

1/4 teaspoon salt

1/4 teaspoon freshly ground black pepper

1/8 teaspoon freshly grated nutmeg

4 tablespoons yogurt

1. Bring 2 quarts of water to a boil and add a generous pinch of salt. Add the watercress, turn the heat down and simmer for 5 minutes. Drain and reserve.

2. Put the stock, watercress, sherry, cornstarch, honey, milk or half-and-half, salt, pepper, and nutmeg into a blender or food processor and blend until smooth.

3. Pour the soup into a saucepan and bring to a boil. Turn down the heat and simmer for about 3 minutes or until the soup is creamy.

4. To serve, top each bowl of soup with a spoonful of yogurt.

The Bernards Inn
Bernardsville, New Jersey
Edward Stone
Executive Chef

Soft-Shell Crabs with Linguine & Basil Pesto

Basil Pesto

8 ounces fresh basil leaves

6 whole garlic cloves

4 ounces pine nuts

1 cup extra virgin olive oil

½ cup grated Romano cheese

Put basil leaves in a food processor and pulse 3 or 4 times. Add the garlic and pine nuts. Turn processor on and slowly add olive oil until it is all incorporated. Transfer the pesto to a bowl and fold in the Romano cheese. Reserve.

SERVES 4

4 large soft-shell crabs, cleaned

4 eggs, beaten

4 ounces milk

2 cups canola or peanut oil for frying

¾ cup flour

½ cup bread crumbs

1 pound linguine

12 tablespoons butter

Basil Pesto (see sidebar)

½ cup diced tomatoes

Salt and pepper to taste

Basil leaves

1. Be sure that the crabs are alive shortly before you cook them. To clean soft-shell crabs, first remove the tail, then lift up the pointed sides and, using scissors, remove the feathery gills. Then cut off the eyes and mouth. Inside the opening behind the cut from the eyes and mouth is a bubblelike sack. Remove it.

2. To fry the crabs, heat the oil in a high-sided saucepan to 360°F. While the oil is heating, set up three shallow bowls for breading the crabs—one with flour, one with eggs and milk mixed together, and one with bread crumbs. Immediately before frying, dredge one crab in flour and then dip it in the egg mixture and then in the bread crumbs. Fry the crab in the hot oil for 2 to 3 minutes. Remove and drain on a paper towel. Keep warm. Repeat with each crab.

3. Bring 6 quarts of water to a rapid boil and add a generous pinch of salt. Add pasta and cook for 7 minutes. Drain. Melt the butter in a 4-quart saucepan and toss the hot pasta with the butter. Stir in the pesto, toss, and season with salt and pepper.

4. To serve, divide the pasta into 4 serving plates or bowls. Top each portion with 1 crab and scatter diced tomatoes over the top. Garnish with basil leaves and serve.

Arthur's Landing Restaurant
Weehawken, New Jersey
Steven Singer
Executive Chef

autumn

Fall is the time for cruciferous vegetables—cauliflower, cabbage, and broccoli—which are not only delicious but also good sources of vitamin C and cancer-fighting phytogens. Apples and pears are plentiful, as are pumpkin and hard squashes. Carrots begin to appear along with lima beans. Spinach, lettuce, kale, and arugula reappear for a second season. And there's still more than enough eggplant and zucchini!

savory autumn dishes…

Treat yourself to an autumn vegetable salad. Combine bite-size pieces of cauliflower, broccoli, carrots, zucchini, and yellow squash with chopped parsley and your favorite vinaigrette. Marinate for one hour.

Create a traditional Three Sisters Native American Indian soup with butternut squash, corn, and pinto beans seasoned with cumin and oregano. Add red miso for richness, if desired.

Revive old-fashioned succotash by combining cooked corn with lima beans and sautéed onions.

Shred cabbage, carrots, zucchini, and yellow squash and combine them with slivered scallions. Toss with lemon juice and cold-pressed oil for a confetti slaw.

To make a fall pasta salad, toss cooked shell pasta with broccoli, cauliflower, julienned fennel, toasted pine nuts, and a white wine vinaigrette. Season with herbes de Provence for a lovely salad or, if you prefer, serve it hot as an elegant entrée, but easy on the vinegar.

Roast pumpkin, butternut squash, and carrots. Peel and puree them with sautéed onions and celery and add hot apple juice or fresh cider for a lovely sweet fall soup.

For a delicious apple crisp, in a baking dish combine thinly sliced, peeled Granny Smith apples with flour, cinnamon, and honey. Top with a mixture of rolled oats, cinnamon, maple syrup, flour, and just a bit of corn oil and sea salt. Bake about 45 minutes at 350°F until the top is browned and the juices bubble.

Stuff green peppers with summer's brown rice salsa salad and add fresh corn and sautéed onions. Top with Jack cheese and bake, or just put the tops of the peppers back on and bake at 350°F for 15 minutes. Delicious!

Edibles…Naturally!
Princeton Junction
New Jersey
Alice Miller
Chef/Owner

Spinach & Fennel Salad with Curried Pears & Gorgonzola

Orange-Rosemary Vinaigrette

This dressing enhances roasted beets and makes a simple sauce for fillets of mild-flavored fish, steamed mussels or clams & broiled shrimp or scallops. Or use it to dress a salad of lettuce, sweet onion, and briny feta.

1 cup fresh orange juice

½ teaspoon orange zest, minced

1 teaspoon chopped rosemary leaves

1 teaspoon minced shallots

2 teaspoons champagne vinegar

¼ teaspoon sugar (optional depending on sweetness of the orange juice)

1 teaspoon olive oil

Pinch of salt & black pepper

Whisk together all of the ingredients in a large bowl. Set aside at room temperature for at least 30 minutes to allow the flavors to meld; then cover and refrigerate for up to 1 week.

White Dog Cafe
Philadelphia
Kevin von Klause
Chef/Partner

SERVES 4

For the pears:

¼ cup fresh orange juice

1 tablespoon White Dog Cafe curry powder (page 73) or good-quality madras curry powder

½ teaspoon ground ginger

1 tablespoon plus 1 teaspoon brown sugar

¼ teaspoon salt

¼ teaspoon freshly ground black pepper

¼ cup olive oil

2 ripe pears, halved and cored

For the salad:

6 cups tightly packed, washed, and stemmed spinach leaves

1 small fennel bulb, stalks removed, cored, and thinly sliced

1 small red onion, peeled and sliced into thin rings

¾ cup **Orange-Rosemary Vinaigrette** (see sidebar)

¼ cup hazelnuts skinned and toasted

4 ounces Gorgonzola cheese, crumbled

1. To make the pears, whisk together the orange juice, curry powder, ginger, brown sugar, salt, and pepper in a small bowl. Slowly whisk in the olive oil. Add the pears and toss to coat with the marinade. Let marinate at room temperature for at least 2 hours or cover and refrigerate for up to 2 days.

2. About 30 minutes before you plan to roast the pears, preheat the oven to 400°F.

3. Place the pears, cut sides down in a baking dish; pour the remaining marinade over them. Roast.

4. To make the salad, toss together the spinach, fennel, red onion, and vinaigrette in a large bowl. Divide the salad among 4 chilled plates. Top each salad with a warm pear half, some of the hazelnuts, and some of the Gorgonzola.

Recipe taken from *The White Dog Cafe Cookbook*, published by Running Press, Philadelphia, in press.

mpkin Risotto

Here is comforting risotto, perfect for a brisk autumn or winter day. Though many recipes for pumpkin risotto call for diced pumpkin simmered in chicken broth, we use a sweet-spiced pumpkin broth to capture the elusive delicate pumpkin flavor.

SERVES 6

For the pumpkin broth:

1 tablespoon butter

1 medium onion, peeled and thinly sliced

2 carrots, peeled and thinly sliced

1 celery stalk with leaves, washed and sliced

1 leek, washed, thinly sliced, white and light-green parts only

2 cups canned pumpkin puree

8 cups chicken stock

1 bay leaf

$\frac{1}{2}$ teaspoon whole black peppercorns

4 allspice berries

$\frac{1}{4}$ teaspoon freshly grated nutmeg

$\frac{1}{4}$ cinnamon stick

2 tablespoons pure maple syrup

For the risotto:

$\frac{1}{4}$ cup olive oil

$1\frac{3}{4}$ cups Arborio rice

$1\frac{1}{2}$ cups diced ($\frac{1}{2}$-inch) fresh pumpkin, butternut, or other firm-fleshed squash

$\frac{1}{2}$ cup dry white wine

6 to 7 cups pumpkin broth

1 tablespoon minced fresh sage

2 cups arugula, washed and chopped

$\frac{1}{3}$ cup diced fresh mozzarella

1 teaspoon kosher salt

$\frac{1}{4}$ teaspoon freshly grated black pepper

$\frac{1}{4}$ cup freshly grated Parmigiano-Reggiano ($\frac{3}{4}$ ounce)

3 tablespoons butter

Union Square Cafe
New York
Michael Romano
Executive Chef/Partner

1. In a large saucepan or stockpot, melt the butter over medium heat. Add the onion, carrots, celery, and leek; sauté until tender and moist, about 10 minutes. Stir in the pumpkin puree and continue cooking for 2 to 3 minutes. Add the chicken stock, bay leaf, spices, and maple syrup. Reduce the heat and simmer covered for 45 minutes. Pour the broth through a fine-mesh strainer. To avoid ending up with a thick puree rather than a broth, take care not to mash the vegetables through the strainer.

2. In the same saucepan, heat the pumpkin broth to a simmer.

3. Heat the olive oil over medium heat in a separate, 3-quart heavy saucepan or skillet. Toss in the rice and diced pumpkin and stir with a wooden spoon until coated with oil. Add the white wine and stir constantly until the rice has absorbed all the wine. Ladle ½ cup of hot pumpkin broth into the pan and stir until it is absorbed. Continue with the rest of the broth, adding ½ cup at a time and letting each addition be absorbed completely into the rice before adding more liquid. The constant stirring allows the rice to release its starch into the cooking liquid, resulting in the characteristic risotto creaminess. The grains of rice should be al dente. Count on approximately 20 to 25 minutes for the rice to cook.

4. Finish by stirring in the sage, arugula, mozzarella, salt, pepper, and half the Parmigiano. Swirl in the butter. Spoon into warm bowls, sprinkle with the remaining Parmigiano, and serve immediately.

Recipe taken from *The Union Square Cafe Cookbook*, published by HarperCollins, New York, 1994.

Country Bread & Roasted Vegetable Salad

The next time you see a nice crusty day-old loaf of bread at your bakery, pick it up and try this hearty, healthful panzanella, or bread salad. The better the bread you use, the better your salad will be: we make it with leftover country-style sourdough. We think the salad is best when eaten just after it is mixed together. However, to work ahead, you can prepare the vegetables and bread a day in advance and then combine them just before serving.

SERVES 4

4 cups cubed (1-inch) country-style bread

1 red bell pepper, diced

1 yellow bell pepper, diced

1 red onion, peeled and diced

2 plum tomatoes, each cut in eight wedges

1 small eggplant, diced

2 teaspoons dried basil

1 teaspoon dried oregano

1 teaspoon dried thyme

½ cup extra virgin olive oil

2 tablespoons balsamic vinegar

1 tablespoon fresh lemon juice

¾ teaspoon salt

½ teaspoon freshly ground black pepper

1. Preheat the oven to 475°F.

2. Spread the cubed bread on a baking sheet. Toast in the oven until crisp, about 5 minutes. Reserve.

3. Meanwhile, combine the bell peppers, red onion, tomatoes, eggplant, basil, oregano, thyme, and half of the olive oil in a large bowl. Toss well to coat the vegetables lightly with the herbs and oil. Spread the vegetables in a single layer on 2 baking sheets. Roast until cooked through and just starting to brown, 10 to 15 minutes. Let cool to room temperature.

4. Combine the toasted bread cubes and roasted vegetables in a large mixing bowl. Add the remaining ¼ cup olive oil, vinegar, lemon juice, salt, and pepper; toss to mix well. Serve immediately or cover and hold for up to 6 hours at room temperature to allow the flavors to meld and the bread to soften slightly.

The Way We Do It: We add fresh basil leaves, parsley, arugula, and baby spinach to the salad just before serving. We also like to toss in some crumbled goat cheese, Gorgonzola, or shavings of Parmesan.

Recipe taken from *The White Dog Cafe Cookbook*, published by Running Press, Philadelphia, in press.

White Dog Cafe
Philadelphia
Kevin von Klause
Chef/Partner

Organic Greens with Tomato-Basil Vinaigrette & Pine Nut Crisps

SERVES 6

6 ounces mesclun greens or any combination of local baby lettuces

For the vinaigrette:

2 small shallots (or ½ small red onion), peeled and finely chopped

Juice of ½ lemon

2 teaspoons balsamic vinegar

4 tablespoons extra virgin olive oil (highest quality)

Salt and pepper to taste

2 medium ripe tomatoes, peeled, seeded, and diced small

2 tablespoons fresh basil, chopped coarsely

For the pine nut crisps:

1 pound Italian Asiago cheese, grated

1 teaspoon butter

2 ounces pine nuts

1. To make the vinaigrette, stir together the shallots, lemon juice, and vinegar. Whisk in the olive oil in a slow, steady stream. Add tomatoes and basil and season with salt and pepper.

2. To make the crisps, melt the butter in a nonstick pan over medium heat. The melted butter should just coat the bottom of the pan. Remove any excess butter if necessary. Spread a very fine layer of the grated cheese in the pan in a 3-inch circle. Sprinkle a pinchful of pine nuts in the center. Cook until the cheese has melted and dried out, forming a crunchy crust with golden edges. Flip the crisp over with a spatula and cook a few more seconds until golden. Lay the crisp on a paper towel to drain and cool. Continue until you have made 12 crisps.

3. To serve, toss the greens with the vinaigrette, mound in the center of each plate, and top with one or two crisps.

The Forrestal
Princeton, New Jersey
Yves Vacheresse
Executive Chef

Organic Bean & Roasted Beet Salad with Curry-Infused Oil

Curry-Infused Oil

*MUST BE MADE 3 DAYS
IN ADVANCE*

2 tablespoons ground curry

2 teaspoons spring water

1 cup grape-seed oil

Place the curry powder with water in a blender and make a paste. Add the grape-seed oil and blend until smooth. Put mixture in a plastic container, cover, and allow to sit for 3 days. Skim off the oil and strain it through a fine sieve. Discard the curry paste.

SERVES 4

1 pound beets, scrubbed and trimmed leaving 1-inch stems

1 teaspoon of grape-seed oil

1 pound of green or yellow wax beans

Sea salt and freshly ground pepper

Juice of 1 lemon

Curry-Infused Oil (see sidebar)

1. Preheat oven to 350°F.

2. Rub the beets with grape-seed oil and place in shallow pan. Cover the bottom of the pan with water and bake for approximately 1 hour or until a knife will slide easily into the largest beet. When cool enough to handle, peel the beets and julienne them.

3. Trim the beans and steam or blanch them until al dente.

4. To prepare the salad, toss the beets and beans with a drizzle of curry oil, lemon juice, and salt and pepper. Serve as a light appetizer or entrée accompanied by whole wheat couscous.

Church Street Bistro
Lambertville, New Jersey
David G. Kiser
Chef/Proprietor

Duck with Roasted Grapes, Figs & Shallots

This is also delicious with duck liver paste on grilled bread for the truly adventurous.

SERVES 4

12 large French shallots, peeled and cut in quarters

Kosher salt and pepper

3 tablespoons extra virgin olive oil

1 tablespoon balsamic vinegar

10 black mission figs

1 bunch black Isabel or red flame grapes

Fresh thyme

1 to 1½ cups zinfandel wine

4 Long Island duck breasts, trimmed and seasoned

2 teaspoons canola oil

1. Toss the shallots with a pinch of kosher salt and pepper, olive oil, and balsamic vinegar. Put in a medium-size crock and bake at 375°F for 20 minutes.

2. Slice the figs in half, and cut the grapes into small bunches leaving the stems on. Add the figs and grapes to the shallots and season with a bit more salt and pepper. Place a few sprigs of thyme on top of the mixture and pour 1 to 1½ cups of zinfandel over everything. Return to oven and bake for 35 to 45 minutes or until figs and shallots are tender and much of the red wine has been absorbed.

3. To sauté the duck breasts, score the skin side with a sharp knife in a crosshatch pattern. Be sure not to cut into the meat. Heat the canola oil in a sauté pan until very hot but not smoking. Put the breast in the pan, skin side down, and sauté over medium-high heat for 4 to 5 minutes until the skin has browned. Turn over and continue to cook for 4 to 5 more minutes. The breast should be medium rare. The duck breasts may also be grilled.

4. Spoon a portion of shallots, figs, and grapes over each duck breast and serve with any excess juices.

ACROSS THE STREET

444 EAST 91 STREET

Across the Street
New York
Seen Lippert
Executive Chef

Roast Leg of Lamb with Vanilla & Thyme

Don't be put off by the outlandish combination of flavors. Vanilla is savory and aromatic, as are many other spices. The only reason we don't include it in our general spice repertoire is that we've learned to associate it exclusively with desserts. In other parts of the world, using vanilla in meat dishes is not uncommon. You will enjoy watching your guests try to place a familiar flavor in an unfamiliar context. Bourbon vanilla beans are considered the best, so try to get them.

The Rainbow Room
New York
Waldy Malouf
Chef/Director

SERVES 6 TO 8 DEPENDING ON THE SIZE OF THE LEG OF LAMB

1 leg of lamb, preferably with hipbone removed, trimmed, and tied (save the bone and trimmings for stock)

For the lamb:

2 teaspoons chopped thyme leaves

1 bourbon vanilla bean or 2 ordinary vanilla beans, split and scraped

1 teaspoon freshly ground pepper

2 teaspoons kosher salt

4 tablespoons olive oil

4 cloves garlic, peeled and sliced

2 medium onions, peeled and sliced

2 medium carrots, peeled and sliced

2 medium stalks celery, sliced

For the sauce:

2 tablespoons unsalted butter

2 tablespoons flour

1 cup good-quality dry white wine

4 cups **Lamb Stock** (see sidebar on next page)

½ vanilla bean, scrapings and pod

1 large sprig thyme

Juice of ½ lemon

Coarse salt and freshly ground pepper

1. Preheat oven to 400°F.

2. Combine the thyme leaves, vanilla, pepper, and salt. Reserve the thyme stems and vanilla pod.

3. Rub the meat all over with this herb-and-spice mixture and then with 2 tablespoons of olive oil.

4. Toss the garlic, onion, carrot, celery, thyme stems, and vanilla pod with the remaining 2 tablespoons of olive oil and lay them in a large roasting pan.

Lamb Stock

4 pounds lamb trimmings and bones—use the meat trimmings and hipbone to make lamb stock. Ask your butcher for more lamb bones so you have a total of approximately 4 pounds.

1 medium carrot, sliced

1 stalk celery, roughly sliced

1 medium onion, peeled and roughly sliced

Herb sachet: using cotton string, tie together in a double layer of damp cheesecloth:

> *1 teaspoon dried thyme*
> *1 bay leaf*
> *4 stems parsley*

Preheat oven to 450°F. Brown the bones and vegetables by putting them in the oven on a baking sheet with a little vegetable oil for about 1 hour.

Put the browned bones, vegetables, and herb sachet in a large pot and cover with cold water by 1 inch. Bring to a boil and skim. Turn down the heat and simmer for 4 to 5 hours.

Strain the stock and degrease the stock either by using a degreasing cup (available at cooking stores) or by chilling the stock and scraping the solidified fat off the top. Boil the stock to reduce it and to concentrate the flavors.

5. Set the meat, top side down, on the bed of vegetables and roast for 1 hour and 15 minutes to 2 hours, turning it once halfway through. Check for doneness by inserting an instant-read thermometer into the meatiest portion of the leg. It should read 145°F for medium rare.

6. Remove the meat to a platter, cover with foil, and allow it to rest in a warm place for at least 20 minutes. While the meat is resting, you can make the sauce.

7. Make the sauce on top of the stove in the roasting pan. First, pour off all the fat. Then, over medium-low heat, melt the butter in the pan and stir in the flour. Stir constantly for 3 to 4 minutes.

8. Add the wine and stir until smooth. Reduce until the mixture is almost dry.

9. Stir in the stock and bring the mixture to a boil.

10. Transfer the sauce to a saucepan and add the vanilla bean and thyme.

11. Bring the sauce to a boil and simmer over medium-high heat, skimming off foam or scum, until the sauce is reduced to approximately 2 cups.

12. Pour the sauce through a strainer and season to taste with lemon juice and salt and pepper.

13. Carve the lamb into thin slices perpendicular to the bone. Arrange on a platter and garnish with fresh thyme and the sauce. Serve remaining sauce in a sauceboat.

Curry-Roasted Vegetables with Indian Cheese Dumplings

Although curry powders abound on every supermarket shelf, you'll find that making your own is well worth the time and expense. The exquisite layers of flavor achieved with homemade curry powder dance circles around flat supermarket brands. We make this dish as part of a vegetarian feast served every fall to celebrate Mahatma Gandhi's birthday. The Indian cheese dumplings help to cool the fire of the curry. However, if you're pressed for time, a dollop of plain yogurt will do.

SERVES 4

¼ cup extra virgin olive oil

2 cups finely diced white onion

¼ cup minced garlic

2 tablespoons minced fresh ginger

2 tablespoons White Dog Cafe curry powder (page 73) or good-quality madras curry powder

1 teaspoon cumin seed

1 teaspoon fennel seed

1 teaspoon fenugreek seed

2 cups canned chopped tomatoes

1 teaspoon salt

¼ teaspoon hot red pepper flakes or to taste

Pinch of freshly ground black pepper

1 pound red-skin potatoes, cut into ½-inch wedges

¼ pound green beans (about 1 cup), trimmed

1 small eggplant (1 pound), cut into ¾-inch dice

3 large carrots, peeled and roll cut (see sidebar on next page)

4 ribs celery, cut on a bias into 2-inch pieces

Indian Cheese Dumplings (see sidebar on next page)

1. Heat the olive oil in a large sauté pan set over medium-high heat until it shimmers. Add the onion and cook until translucent, about 5 minutes. Add the garlic and ginger and cook for 2 minutes more. Add the curry powder, cumin seed, fennel seed, and fenugreek seed. Cook for 1 minute, stirring constantly. Add the chopped tomatoes, salt, hot pepper flakes, and black pepper. Bring to a simmer and remove from the heat. Allow to cool slightly. The curry can be prepared ahead of time up to this point. Cool to room temperature, cover, and refrigerate for up to 2 days before proceeding with step 2.

2. Preheat oven to 400°F.

3. Spread the vegetables evenly on 2 large baking sheets. Pour the curry sauce over the vegetables. Toss to coat

White Dog Cafe
Philadelphia
Kevin von Klause
Chef/Partner

How to make a roll cut

To roll-cut carrots, place a peeled carrot on a cutting board. Angle your knife at a 45° angle and make a diagonal cut to remove the stem end of the carrot. Keeping the knife in the same position, roll the carrot 180° (a half turn) and make another diagonal cut. This will produce a triangular wedge of carrot with one rounded side. Repeat until the entire carrot has been cut.

Indian Cheese Dumplings

1½ cups plain yogurt

¼ cup chopped cilantro

Salt and freshly ground black pepper to taste

Line a colander or strainer with cheesecloth or a coffee filter and set over a bowl. Place the yogurt in the strainer and refrigerate for 6 hours or until the yogurt is drained of excess moisture. It should be firm and compact. Remove the yogurt to a bowl and stir in the cilantro, salt, and pepper. Shape into 8 round dumplings and serve or cover and refrigerate for up to 3 days.

them well with the sauce. Roast the vegetables until cooked through and starting to brown, 20 to 30 minutes. Stir the vegetables once or twice while they are roasting. Serve immediately or cool to room temperature. Cover and refrigerate for up to 2 days. Reheat before serving.

White Dog Cafe Curry Powder

Make curry powder in small batches and keep it tightly covered for maximum flavor and freshness.

MAKES ABOUT ½ CUP

½ teaspoon hot red chili flakes

1 teaspoon black mustard seed

1 tablespoon freshly ground black pepper

1 tablespoon ground cinnamon

1 tablespoon ground fennel seed

1 tablespoon ground cumin

1 teaspoon ground cardamom

1 teaspoon ground cloves

1 bay leaf

1 tablespoon ground fenugreek seed

1 tablespoon ground coriander

1 teaspoon turmeric

Combine all of the ingredients in a small bowl and mix well. Store tightly covered in an airtight container for up to 1 month.

Recipes taken from *The White Dog Cafe Cookbook*, published by Running Press, Philadelphia, in press.

Grilled Salmon with Garden Slaw & White Corn Vinaigrette

White Corn Vinaigrette

3 shallots, peeled and finely chopped

4 ears of fresh white corn, cooked and then kernels cut from cobs

1 tablespoon sherry wine vinegar

½ cup canola oil

1 tablespoon Italian flat-leaf parsley, chopped

Salt and pepper to taste

Combine the shallots, cooked corn, sherry wine vinegar, canola oil, and Italian parsley in a blender and blend until smooth. Season to taste with salt and pepper. Add additional oil and vinegar if the sauce seems dry. Reserve to use as a garnish for the fish.

For the salmon:

6 seven-ounce salmon fillets

White Corn Vinaigrette (see sidebar)

For the garden slaw:

2 small bell peppers, of different color, cut in thin strips

3 medium carrots, peeled and julienned

½ small red cabbage, sliced very thinly

1 dozen sprigs of cilantro

1 small jicama, peeled and julienned

3 tablespoons crème fraîche or sour cream

Soy sauce to taste

1 tablespoon rice wine vinegar

1. The salmon can be grilled or broiled. Prepare a grill or preheat broiler 30 minutes before cooking.

2. Make the vinaigrette.

3. To make the garden slaw, mix crème fraîche, rice wine vinegar, and soy sauce until well blended. Reserve. Combine the peppers, carrots, cabbage, cilantro, and jicama together and toss with the reserved sauce. Set aside.

4. To cook the fish, rub both sides of the fillet with a little olive oil and season with salt and pepper. Grill close to the flame for 3 to 5 minutes on each side preferably to medium rare. For broiling, set the rack 2 inches from the heating element and proceed as with grilling.

5. Serve the fish with the garden slaw and garnish with the white corn vinaigrette.

The Forrestal
Princeton, New Jersey
Yves Vacheresse
Executive Chef

Japanese Eggplant with Anchovy & Mint

This is also delicious made ahead and served as part of an antipasto.

SERVES 4

4 medium Japanese eggplants

Salt and pepper

Olive oil

For the dressing:

2 shallots, peeled and minced

Juice of 2 lemons

1 teaspoon lemon zest, minced

8 anchovies, rinsed, filleted, and chopped

½ to ¾ cup extra virgin olive oil

15 to 20 leaves fresh mint, minced

Salt and pepper

1. Leaving the stem end intact, make ¼-inch-thick vertical slices from the stem through the bottom of the eggplant. Spread slightly, like a fan, and season with salt, pepper, and a drizzle of olive oil.

2. Grill the eggplant over a slow fire for about 20 to 25 minutes or roast in a 450°F oven for 15 to 20 minutes or until very soft.

3. Stir together the lemon juice, lemon zest, anchovies, and mint and whisk in the olive oil in a slow, steady stream. Season to taste with salt and pepper.

4. Place the grilled eggplant on a plate and spoon dressing over the top. Serve warm or at room temperature.

ACROSS THE STREET

444 EAST 91 STREET

Across the Street
New York
Seen Lippert
Executive Chef

Roast Saddle of Venison with Wild Huckleberries

There are many fine stocks available at gourmet shops and supermarkets. Even your butcher might carry some. Look for products described as a glace. A glace is a very rich reduced stock.

SERVES 10

A saddle of venison, bone in, trimmed and tied—your butcher can do this for you

Marinade (see sidebar on next page)

For roasting the meat:

Vegetable oil to rub the meat

1 medium onion, peeled and cut in a ¼-inch dice

1 stalk celery, cut in a ¼-inch dice

1 carrot, peeled and cut in a ¼-inch dice

4 cloves garlic, peeled and chopped

5 or 6 parsley stems, chopped

1 tablespoon crushed juniper berries

For the sauce:

2 tablespoons unsalted butter

1½ pints huckleberries or black or red currants (jarred or frozen if fresh berries are not available)

2 tablespoons flour

2 cups apple cider

2 tablespoons red wine vinegar

4 cups rich meat stock

Kosher salt and freshly ground pepper

Chopped parsley

2 days before cooking:

1. Make the marinade. Add the venison, cover, and marinate in the refrigerator for at least 48 hours, turning twice.

The day of the meal:

2. Take the venison out of the refrigerator at least 2 hours before cooking to allow the meat to come to room temperature.

3. Preheat oven to 450°F.

The Rainbow Room
New York
Waldy Malouf
Chef/Director

Marinade

1 bottle dry red wine

1 small onion, peeled and sliced

4 shallots, peeled and sliced

2 cloves garlic, peeled and sliced

2 bay leaves

1 teaspoon dried thyme

1 tablespoon crushed juniper berries

1 tablespoon peppercorns

In a large nonreactive bowl, combine all the ingredients.

4. Remove the venison from the marinade and pat it dry with paper towels. Rub the meat all over with a little vegetable oil and season it with salt and freshly ground pepper.

5. Put the venison in a roasting pan. Roast for 20 minutes.

6. Combine the onion, celery, carrot, garlic, parsley, and juniper berries and add them to the pan, spreading them in an even layer and pushing some under the meat.

7. Turn the oven down to 400°F and roast the meat for another 40 minutes.

8. Remove the meat from the oven and cover with foil to keep it warm while you make the sauce.

9. To make the sauce, add the butter and 1 pint of the huckleberries to the vegetables in the roasting pan. Cook and stir them over medium heat on top of the stove until they are soft, adding a little butter if they are dry. When the vegetables are soft, sprinkle them with the flour. Stir well and cook for 2 or 3 minutes.

10. Add the cider and deglaze the pan.

11. Transfer the mixture into a saucepan and cook over medium-high heat, stirring frequently until it is reduced to the consistency of a thick marmalade.

12. Stir in the vinegar and cook for 2 or 3 minutes. Add the stock and stir well. Bring the mixture to a boil and cook until the liquid is reduced by half.

13. Strain the sauce into a clean saucepan; press out all the liquid but do not push any solids through. Bring the sauce to a boil, skim off any fat or scum, and season the sauce with salt and pepper.

14. When the whole loin has been carved, turn the roast upside down and using your knife, scoop out the whole fillets. Slice them into 1-inch-thick medallions.

15. Put the slices on a platter. Spoon a little sauce over the meat and sprinkle the platter with the reserved huckleberries and a little chopped parsley.

Curried Apple Bisque with Minted Yogurt

In the fall when the cider is first pressed, we use it as a stock for this savory-sweet bisque. The soup is very low in fat but full of flavors that even kids like. Our homemade curry powder gives it a little heat that we like to temper with a splash of cool minted yogurt.

Minted Yogurt

MAKES 1 CUP

1 cup plain low-fat yogurt

2 teaspoons fresh mint, minced

¼ teaspoon salt, optional

Combine all ingredients. Store covered in the refrigerator until ready to use. Can be stored for up to 1 week.

SERVES 6

2 tablespoons olive oil

1 large yellow onion, peeled and diced (about 2 cups)

2 tablespoons minced fresh ginger

1 tablespoon minced garlic

1 tablespoon plus 1 teaspoon White Dog Cafe curry powder (page 73) or good-quality madras curry powder

5 Granny Smith apples, peeled, cored, diced (about 6 cups)

3 cups apple cider

1 teaspoon salt

1 recipe **Minted Yogurt,** for serving (see sidebar)

1. Heat the oil in a large saucepan placed over medium heat. Add the onion and cook until soft and translucent, about 5 minutes. Add the ginger and garlic and cook for another 2 to 3 minutes or until soft. Do not let garlic brown or it will give the bisque a bitter flavor.

2. Stir in the curry powder and cook, tossing with the onion mixture for about 1 minute; scrape the bottom of the pan so the mixture doesn't scorch. Add the apples, cider, 2 cups of water, and salt and bring to a boil. Reduce the heat to low and simmer until the apples are completely soft, about 30 minutes.

3. Puree the mixture in batches in a food processor, blender, or food mill. Return to the saucepan and season with salt to taste. Serve warm, or let cool to room temperature, cover, and refrigerate for up to 3 days (or freeze for up to 3 months). Top each portion with a generous dollop of minted yogurt.

Other Ways to Do It: You can substitute any ripe cooking apple such as Rome, Cortland, winesap, or yellow delicious in this recipe with excellent results. When you use red apples, leave the skins on. They give the bisque a lovely copper color. If you can't make your own curry powder, use a good-quality madras curry powder such as Sun brand.

Recipe taken from *The White Dog Cafe Cookbook*, published by Running Press, Philadelphia, in press.

White Dog Cafe
Philadelphia
Kevin von Klause
Chef/Partner

Curried Squash-Apple Soup

SERVES 10

4 tablespoons butter

2 medium onions, peeled and chopped

2 garlic cloves, peeled and minced

2 to 4 tablespoons curry powder

1 Granny Smith apple, peeled, cored, and chopped

2 pounds butternut squash, peeled and chopped

4 to 6 cups vegetable stock or chicken stock

1 tablespoon tawny port wine

2 teaspoons kosher salt

1 teaspoon freshly ground black pepper

¼ cup pine nuts, lightly toasted

1. Heat the butter in a heavy 5-quart pot over medium heat. Add the onions and sauté until translucent, about 10 minutes. Add the garlic and curry powder and cook, stirring for 1 minute. Stir in the apple, squash, and stock. Cover and cook until the squash is soft, about 35 minutes.

2. Remove the soup from the heat and, when slightly cooled, puree it in batches in a food processor. Pour the soup back into the pot and stir in the port and salt and pepper.

3. To serve, reheat the soup, ladle into soup bowls, and garnish with pine nuts.

The Bernards Inn
Bernardsville, New Jersey
Edward Stone
Executive Chef

Shrimp Risotto with Cucumber & Jalapeño

Here's a refreshing risotto variation substituting fresh cucumber juice for chicken or fish broth. The cucumber flavor is a sweet complement to the shrimp and softens the punch of the spicy jalapeño.

SERVES 4 TO 6

6 cups cucumber juice or 8 cucumbers peeled, blended and strained to yield 6 cups juice

2 tablespoons olive oil

3/4 pound cleaned medium shrimp, split lengthwise

1/4 cup minced jalapeño, seeded

1 teaspoon kosher salt

1/8 teaspoon freshly ground black pepper

1 tablespoon minced shallot

1 3/4 cup Arborio rice

1 cup white wine

2 tablespoons butter

3/4 cup chopped cilantro

Juice of 1 lime

1. In a small saucepan bring the cucumber juice to a simmer, remove from the heat, and reserve.

2. In a 3-quart saucepan or skillet, heat 1 tablespoon of the olive oil. Add the shrimp and jalapeño, season with 1/4 teaspoon salt and half the pepper, and sauté 2 minutes over high heat. Remove from pan and reserve.

3. Return the pan to a medium flame, add the remaining teaspoon of oil, and cook the shallots, scraping up any cooked bits from the bottom of the pan. Toss in the rice and stir with a wooden spoon until the rice is coated with oil. Add the white wine and stir constantly over medium heat until all the wine is absorbed by the rice. Ladle 1/2 cup of the warm cucumber juice into the pan and stir until it is absorbed. Continue with the rest of the juice, adding 1/2 cup at a time and letting each addition be absorbed completely into the rice before adding more liquid. The constant stirring allows the rice to release its starch into the cooking liquid, resulting in the characteristic risotto creaminess. The grains of rice should be al dente. Count on about 20 to 25 minutes for the rice to cook.

4. Add the shrimp and jalapeño and swirl the butter. Season with the remaining salt and pepper. Finish by stirring in the chopped cilantro and lime juice. Serve immediately.

Recipe taken from *The Union Square Cafe Cookbook*, published by HarperCollins, New York, 1994.

Union Square Cafe
New York
Michael Romano
Executive Chef/Partner

Salade de Marche

SERVES 4

4 small heads or bunches of various greens such as butter lettuce, arugula, dandelion, mâche, edible flowers, and herbs, washed and dried

¼ cup champagne vinegar

1 teaspoon Dijon mustard

3 tablespoons fresh orange juice

½ cup extra virgin olive oil

1 teaspoon grated orange rind

Fine sea salt and freshly ground pepper, to taste

1. To make the vinaigrette, whisk together the vinegar, mustard, and orange juice. Whisking constantly, add the olive oil in a slow steady stream until emulsified. Finish with grated orange rind.

2. Toss the greens, herbs, and flowers with the vinaigrette and add salt and pepper to taste.

Church Street Bistro
Lambertville, New Jersey
David G. Kiser
Chef/Proprietor

winter

Winter vegetables are warming and nutritious. While harvested in the fall, they can be stored for use throughout the winter. They provide plenty of vitamins A, B, and C as well as folic acid and potassium. Cooked onions, carrots, potatoes, and squashes are naturally sweet and satisfy cravings for desserts. And don't be afraid of burdock, rutabaga, celeriac, and kohlrabi!

to brighten a gray winter day…

Grate kohlrabi and celeriac (celery root) for winter salads.

To create a hearty winter stew, stew burdock root with carrots, onions, and chickpeas. Serve over brown rice for a winter-warming and nutritious entrée. Or, for extra drama, serve it in a scooped-out and baked pumpkin, carefully scraping some cooked pumpkin from the inside when serving.

Puree roasted carrots, rutabagas, turnips, and parsnips and thin with a white miso broth for a rich, warming roasted winter vegetable soup.

To make oven-roasted potatoes, peel and cube white or sweet potatoes and toss with a small amount of oil and chopped fresh rosemary or sage. Roast at 375°F until well browned.

Trim—but don't peel—beets, leaving a little stem on the end. Lightly oil and roast for one hour at 400°F. Be sure to wear gloves when peeling beets!

Shred white and red cabbage and carrots and toss them together with your favorite vinaigrette for a confetti slaw.

For a hearty onion soup, slowly cook sliced onions to caramelize them. Add a touch of soy sauce to deepen the color and stir in vegetable broth. Serve with homemade croutons.

Bake russet, Idaho, or sweet potatoes and top with a mixture of half Dijon mustard and half nonfat yogurt. Or top with chile and grated cheese, if you like.

Edibles…Naturally!
Princeton Junction
New Jersey
Alice Miller
Chef/Owner

Creamy White Bean & Turnip Soup with Roasted Beets

SERVES 12

Cooking Navy Beans

The day before making the soup, sort through the beans and discard any small stones or sticks. Rinse the beans under running water, place them in a large bowl, and cover them by 3 inches with cold water. Allow the beans to soak overnight.

The next day, pour off the soaking water and put the beans in a large pot. Cover the beans by 3 inches with fresh cold water and bring to a boil.

Skim off any foam. Turn down the heat and simmer covered for 45 minutes. If water drops below the level of the beans, add more water to cover. After 45 minutes, check to see if the beans are soft. If not, continue to simmer until they have finished cooking. Drain water off the beans.

The Forrestal
Princeton, New Jersey
Yves Vacheresse
Executive Chef

For the soup:

1 pound navy beans, cooked (see sidebar)

4 tablespoons unsalted butter

2 medium leeks, cleaned, chopped finely (white part only)

2 russett potatoes, peeled and diced

6 medium turnips, peeled and diced

2 quarts chicken stock

1 cup heavy cream

Salt and pepper to taste

For the beets:

2 tablespoons butter

6 small beets, peeled and cut in ¼-inch sticks

¼ cup water

Salt and pepper to taste

1. To make the soup, melt 4 tablespoons of butter in a medium-size sauté pan. Add the leeks and cook over low heat until they are translucent. Add the potatoes, turnips, and stock and bring to a boil. Reduce the heat and let simmer until the vegetables are soft, about 20 minutes. Add the heavy cream and white beans and simmer for 10 more minutes. Everything should be very soft.

2. Strain the soup mixture, reserving the solids and liquid separately. Puree the solids in a food processor or blender. Add back ⅔ to ¾ of the liquid. Check the consistency. If the soup is too thick, add more liquid. Season to taste with salt and pepper.

3. To cook the beets, preheat the oven to 350°F. Melt 2 tablespoons of butter in a small ovenproof pan. Sauté the beets for a few minutes. Add the water, bring it to a boil, and boil on high heat until most of the water has evaporated. Season with salt and pepper and place in a 350°F oven for 45 minutes. Stir the beets every 10 minutes. Beets should be soft with a dark skin.

4. To serve, heat the soup, pour into serving bowls, and garnish with a pinchful of warm beets.

Braised Rabbit with Beets & Yukon Gold Mashed Potatoes

This recipe also works well with a large (3½-pound) chicken.

SERVES 4

For the potatoes:

Kosher salt (for baking the potatoes)

2 pounds Yukon Gold potatoes, washed and not peeled

½ cup milk or cream

4 tablespoons unsalted butter

Sea salt and black or white pepper

⅛ teaspoon nutmeg, freshly grated

For the rabbit:

2 tablespoons olive oil

1 whole rabbit, cut into 9 pieces (2 legs cut in 2, 2 shoulders, 1 back cut in 2, rib section)

Celery salt and white pepper (or sea salt and black pepper)

6 ounces celeriac (celery root), peeled and coarsely chopped

6 ounces celery, coarsely chopped

6 ounces carrots, peeled and coarsely chopped

6 ounces onion, peeled and coarsely chopped

6 cloves garlic, peeled and coarsely chopped

1 cup white wine

1 cup chicken broth

¼ small bunch fresh thyme

1 sprig rosemary

2 bay leaves

1 tablespoon butter, cold

For the beets:

1¼ pounds small beets—preferably a mix of golden, red, and striped—washed and not peeled

2 tablespoons butter

½ teaspoon brown sugar

1 teaspoon chopped flat-leaf parsley

1. Preheat oven to 375°F.

2. Line a roasting pan with ½ inch of kosher salt. Place the potatoes on the salt and bake until a knife will slide easily into them, about 1 hour. Set them aside.

Windows on the World
New York
Frederic Kieffer
Private Dining Chef

3. Heat 2 tablespoons olive oil over high heat in a large saucepan that has a cover. Season the rabbit with salt and pepper. When the pan is hot but not smoking, sauté the rabbit until each piece is brown on all sides. Remove to a plate.

4. Lower the flame and in the same saucepan add the celeriac, celery, carrots, onions, and garlic and brown lightly, approximately 7 to 10 minutes. Place the rabbit on top of the vegetables and add the wine, broth, thyme, rosemary, and bay leaves. Bring the mixture to a rolling boil and immediately turn down the heat. Simmer the rabbit and vegetables on very low heat, with the cover on, for 45 minutes to 1 hour.

5. While the rabbit is cooking, trim the greens off the beets leaving a short stem on the very small ones. Using a separate pot for each color beet, fill each pot with enough water to completely cover the beets. Bring water to a boil and add a generous pinch of salt. Add the beets and boil for approximately 10 minutes or until a paring knife slides through the largest beet without much resistance. The beets should be slightly firm. Remove the beets from the water and cool slightly. To remove the beet skins, rub them with a cloth towel. Cut the peeled beets into small wedges or leave them whole if they are very small.

6. Peel the baked potatoes and mash them with a hand masher. Heat the milk to almost a boil and incorporate the butter and hot milk into the potatoes. Season to taste with sea salt, pepper, and nutmeg. Put in a serving dish and keep warm.

7. Remove the rabbit pieces from the saucepan and put them into a serving dish. Strain the sauce and return it to the pan. Bring the sauce to a boil and reduce it to ¾ cup of liquid. Season with salt and pepper and whisk in 1 tablespoon of cold butter. Pour the hot sauce over the rabbit and cover to keep warm.

8. Melt 2 tablespoons of butter in a sauté pan. Add the beets, brown sugar, and a pinch of salt and pepper. Cook until the butter and sugar are thick enough to coat the beets, approximately 2 to 3 minutes. Top with a small amount of chopped parsley.

9. Surround the rabbit with beets and serve with mashed potatoes.

roccoli Rabe on Toast

SERVES 4

4 slices levain bread, sliced ½-inch thick. (Levain is a French sourdough bread. You may substitute other country sourdough breads.)

Extra virgin olive oil

1 whole clove garlic, peeled

1 bunch broccoli rabe, washed and cut into 1-inch pieces

4 cloves garlic, peeled and minced

1 lemon

¼ teaspoon red pepper flakes

¼ pound Parmesan cheese

1. Heat a sauté pan and lightly coat it with olive oil. Fry the bread on both sides to golden brown. Rub one side of each slice of bread with a whole garlic clove.

2. In the same pan, add a bit more olive oil and sauté the broccoli rabe until soft. Add the hot pepper flakes, minced garlic, salt, and pepper.

3. When the broccoli rabe is tender, season it with a squeeze of fresh lemon juice.

4. Spoon the broccoli over the toast and grate or shave fresh Parmesan over the top.

ACROSS THE STREET

444 EAST 91 STREET

Across the Street
New York
Seen Lippert
Executive Chef

Winter Split Pea Soup

Clarified Butter

YIELDS 1½ CUPS

Cut 1 pound of unsalted butter into small pieces and melt in a heavy saucepan over low heat. Don't allow the butter to brown.

Skim the foam off the top with a spoon or a small fine-mesh strainer. Carefully remove the clear-yellow layer with a spoon or small ladle, leaving the milky water and solids at the bottom of the pan. Discard the milky water and solids.

Let the clarified butter cool and store in a jar with a tight-fitting lid.

SERVES 8

2 cups dry green or yellow split peas

6 cups water

1 tablespoon **Clarified Butter** (see sidebar)

1 onion, peeled and chopped

1 rib celery, chopped

1 clove garlic, peeled and minced

2 teaspoons curry powder

1 teaspoon salt

¼ teaspoon freshly ground black pepper

¼ cup dry sherry

7 cups chicken stock or vegetable stock

1 bay leaf

1. Soak the dried split peas in 6 cups of water overnight. Drain the soaking water and rinse the peas.

2. Heat a 3- to 5-quart stock pot to medium-high heat. Add the clarified butter and sauté the onion, celery, and garlic for 5 minutes. Add the curry powder, salt, and pepper and sauté for 2 to 3 more minutes. Add the sherry and stir for 1 minute.

3. Add the split peas, stock, and bay leaf. Bring to a boil. Skim off the foam, turn the heat down, and simmer for 1 hour stirring often.

4. Taste the soup to be sure that the peas are soft and season to taste with salt and pepper.

The Bernards Inn
Bernardsville, New Jersey
Edward Stone
Executive Chef

"*I* am fortunate that my restaurant is situated in the heart of the Garden State. The wealth of fresh organic produce that is available now is a luxury for me. My culinary style is simple and direct. When fresh organic products are plentiful, they enhance all of my dishes. *"*

Edward Stone

Corn & Codfish Chowder

Fish Stock

MAKES 3 QUARTS

4 pounds heads and bones from flavorful whitefish such as striped bass, red snapper, or cod.

2 tablespoons unsalted butter

5 shallots, peeled and sliced

2 stalks celery, sliced

½ pound mushrooms, sliced

1 cup dry white wine

12 parsley stems

1 tablespoon black peppercorns

3 fresh thyme sprigs

(continued next page)

SERVES 10 TO 12 AS A FIRST COURSE, 4 TO 6 AS A MAIN COURSE

4 tablespoons extra virgin olive oil

2 medium onions, peeled, cut in half and sliced thin

4 large ears fresh corn

2 large baking potatoes, peeled, halved lengthwise and sliced thin

1½ pounds cod, sliced 1 inch thick, cut into small pieces

1 tablespoon kosher salt and some freshly ground pepper

2½ cups **Fish Stock** (see sidebars on this page and next)

2½ cups **Chicken Stock** (see next page)

Herb sachet: using cotton string, tie together in a double layer of damp cheesecloth:

> 1 tablespoon black peppercorns
>
> 1 teaspoon dried thyme
>
> 1 bay leaf
>
> 4 or 5 sprigs parsley
>
> 2 cloves garlic, smashed

2½ cups heavy cream

Fresh thyme leaves

1. Heat the olive oil in a heavy-bottomed soup pot, add the onions, and sauté gently until they are translucent and not browned. Cut the kernels from the ears of corn and reserve the cobs. Add the potatoes, half the fish, the corn, and the corn cobs to the pot, season with some salt and pepper, and stir everything together. Add the stocks and the herb sachet and bring the soup to a boil. Turn down the heat and simmer, uncovered, for 30 minutes.

2. Remove the herb sachet and corn cobs from the soup, add the cream, and continue to simmer the soup for another 15 minutes. Cool and refrigerate overnight.

3. Shortly before serving, reheat the soup. Add the remaining fish and let the soup come back to a simmer. Reseason the soup with salt and pepper and let it simmer for 10 minutes or until the fish is cooked through. Ladle into warm bowls and garnish each serving with a pinch of fresh thyme leaves. Serve immediately.

The Rainbow Room
New York
Waldy Malouf
Chef/Director

(Fish Stock, continued)

Fish heads and bones can be obtained from the fish market. Be sure they are fresh and have no unpleasant smell. Check that they have been completely gutted and the gills are removed from the heads. Wash them thoroughly under running water so that they are free of any blood.

Melt the butter in a soup pot and gently cook the shallots, celery, and mushrooms, without allowing them to brown, until they are limp, about 6 to 8 minutes. Add the wine and simmer for 5 minutes to reduce it a bit; then add the fish and seasonings to the pot. Add 14 cups cold water, bring to a boil, and simmer the stock, uncovered, for 45 minutes, stirring once or twice. Strain the stock, let it cool, and pour it into containers for storing or freezing.

Chicken Stock

1 leek, white part and 1 inch green, carefully washed

2 medium carrots, peeled and sliced

2 stalks celery, sliced

1 medium turnip, peeled and sliced

1 medium onion, peeled and sliced

2 cloves garlic, peeled

½ pound mushrooms

2 fresh thyme sprigs or 1 teaspoon dried thyme

2 bay leaves

7 or 8 parsley stems

1 tablespoon black peppercorns

4 pounds chicken backs and necks or thighs and legs, rinsed

1. Put all the vegetables, seasonings, and chicken parts into your largest stockpot. Cover with cold water by 1 inch and bring to a boil. Simmer, with the lid ajar, skimming occasionally, for 4 to 6 hours.

2. Strain the stock and let it cool. Degrease it either by using a degreasing cup (available at cooking stores) or by chilling the stock and scraping the solidified fat off the top. Boil the stock to reduce it and concentrate the flavors. Season with salt and pepper. Pour the cooled stock into containers and refrigerate or freeze it.

Winter Lobster Hash with Lemon Butter & Poached Eggs

SERVES 6

How to poach eggs without an egg poacher

Choose a large round pan with a 3-inch side. Fill the pan with 2 inches of water and a dash of vinegar. Bring the water to a boil and turn down to a very slight simmer. Carefully crack the eggs into the water around the edge of the pan. Poach on a low simmer for 5 to 7 minutes and remove with a slotted spoon.

To hold the eggs for later service, place the poached eggs in a bowl of cold water. To serve, simply drain the cold water and cover the eggs with boiling water to rewarm.

For the hash:

Meat of 2 cooked lobsters (1½ pound each), diced

4 tablespoons unsalted butter

2 tablespoons extra virgin olive oil

1½ pound russett-style potatoes, peeled, cut in a ½-inch dice

1 medium-size red pepper, cut in a ¼-inch dice

1 medium-size green pepper, cut in a ¼-inch dice

1 medium-size red onion, peeled and cut in a ¼-inch dice

For the lemon butter:

½ cup heavy cream

8 tablespoons butter, diced

Juice of ½ lemon

For serving:

6 eggs, poached

Cayenne pepper and salt

1. Melt butter and 1 tablespoon of olive oil together in a large sauté pan. Dry off the diced potatoes by blotting them with paper towels. Sauté the potatoes on medium-high heat. Be sure that the pan can hold them all in a single layer and that they are not crowded. Cook until they are a light golden brown.

2. In a separate pan, sauté the peppers and onions in the remaining olive oil until they are soft and light brown. Add the pepper mixture to the potatoes, stir in the lobster meat, and cook for 4 to 5 minutes.

3. For the lemon butter, bring the heavy cream to a boil. Whisk in the diced butter one piece at a time over medium-high heat. The sauce should be emulsified, which means that the butter and cream are completely combined in a smooth mass with no melted butter visible. Remove from the heat and stir in lemon juice, salt, and cayenne pepper.

4. Poach the eggs.

5. Serve the hash mounded in the center of the plate, topped by a poached egg and a drizzle of lemon butter.

THE FORRESTAL
AT PRINCETON

HOTEL & CONFERENCE CENTER

The Forrestal
Princeton, New Jersey
Yves Vacheresse
Executive Chef

Brussels Sprouts with Mustard & Crème Fraîche

This dish is great with bacon-wrapped monkfish or grilled lamb. Because the vegetable is creamy, no sauce is necessary!

SERVES 4

3 tablespoons pure olive oil

1 large yellow onion, peeled and diced small

1½ pounds fresh brussels sprouts, trimmed and sliced ¼-inch thick

¼ cup water

Kosher salt and black pepper, to taste

1½ cups crème fraîche

¼ cup Dijon mustard

Juice of 1 lemon

1. Heat a 6-quart pot and coat with the olive oil. Add the onion and sauté for 7 to 8 minutes over medium heat.

2. Add the brussels sprouts, water, and a good pinch of salt. Cover and cook for 8 to 10 minutes, or just to done.

3. Uncover and add the crème fraîche, mustard, and lemon juice. Continue cooking for 5 minutes or until the liquid has reduced a bit. It should be creamy and saucelike.

4. Season with salt and pepper to taste and serve.

ACROSS THE STREET

444 EAST 91 STREET

Across the Street
New York
Seen Lippert
Executive Chef

butternut Squash Consommé with Ginger & Scallion Custard

Scallion Custard

3 extra-large egg yolks
(separated from soup)

1 cup heavy cream

1 tablespoon grated fresh
ginger

2 scallions, including green
part, chopped

Kosher salt and freshly
ground pepper

Preheat the oven to 300°F.
Spray the bottom and sides
of six 2-ounce or two
6-ounce ramekins with
nonstick spray. Combine the
3 egg yolks, heavy cream,
ginger, and half of the
scallions and divide it
among the ramekins. Set the
ramekins on a layer of
paper towels in a roasting
pan and add hot water to
come halfway up the sides
of the ramekins. Put the pan
in the oven and bake until
the edges are set and the
custards still quiver just a
little bit in the center when
the pan is shaken, 20 to 25
minutes for the small, 35 to
40 minutes for the larger
custards. Remove the pan
from the oven and leave the
custards in the hot water.
If you are using the fried
ginger, prepare it while the
custards bake.

As with all soups, prepare this a day or two ahead, but make the
custard an hour before serving.

SERVES 6

Equipment: Six 2-ounce or two 6-ounce ramekins
Nonstick spray

For the soup:

3 leeks, white part only

2 stalks celery

1 medium carrot, peeled and sliced

1 medium turnip, peeled and sliced

1 medium parsnip, peeled and sliced

1 small onion, peeled and sliced

1 butternut squash (4½ pounds), sliced in thick rounds,
   unpeeled

6 extra-large eggs separated; reserve 3 yolks for the custard

1 clove garlic, peeled

2 fresh sage leaves

Parsley stems

1 teaspoon fresh thyme leaves

1 clove

1 teaspoon black peppercorns

Kosher salt

Scallion Custard (see sidebar)

Crisp Fried Ginger (see sidebar on next page)

1. Set aside ¼ of the vegetables, including 3 slices of squash.
   Put the remaining vegetables in a large heavy-bottomed
   soup pot.

2. Add 12 cups water to the pot and bring the soup to a
   boil. Simmer the soup over medium-high heat, partially
   covered, for 2 hours.

3. While the soup is cooking, peel and seed the reserved
   squash slices, cut them into fine dice, and reserve ½ cup
   for garnish.

4. You will need to clarify the consommé. The first step is to
   combine the diced squash with the reserved vegetables,
   garlic, sage, parsley, and thyme and process them all in the

Crisp Fried Ginger

Vegetable oil for frying

Flour for dredging

4 tablespoons fresh ginger, peeled, sliced thin, cut into fine strips

Heat about 1½ inches vegetable oil in a saucepan. Put the flour on a plate and toss the fine strips of ginger in it. The ginger strips should be thoroughly coated with flour. Put the ginger in a sieve and shake out any excess flour. When a pinch of flour sizzles and browns in the hot oil, put in the ginger strips and fry them over high heat until they are crisp and brown, 3 or 4 minutes. Drain on paper towels.

RAINBOW!

The Rainbow Room
New York
Waldy Malouf
Chef/Director

food processor until they are finely chopped. Transfer the mixture to a bowl and stir in the clove and peppercorn.

5. Separate the eggs, reserving 3 of the yolks for the ginger custard, and add the whites to the chopped vegetable mixture. Combine well, add 1 cup of cold water, and mix thoroughly. Refrigerate the mixture for at least ½ hour. We will now refer to this mixture as *the clarification mixture*.

6. Strain the soup into a bowl, pressing hard on the solids through the strainer. This will take a little time. You have to coax the liquid out of the vegetables by pressing them against the sides of the strainer and allowing the liquid to run out the middle.

7. To clarify the soup, rinse out the heavy-bottomed soup pot, return the soup to it, and bring it back to a boil. Turn the heat down so the soup is gently simmering. Stirring constantly, add the clarification mixture and, as the soup simmers, continue to stir gently, distributing the mixture throughout the broth, for 15 minutes. The clarification mixture will solidify and form a raft. Put a ladle through the center of the raft to form a hole. Let the soup simmer for one hour, occasionally stirring the soup very gently through the hole. Set a chinois (a very fine mesh strainer) or a strainer lined with a clean dishtowel, several layers of cheesecloth, or a coffee filter over a pot. To remove the soup from the pot, dip the ladle into the hole in the raft, being careful not to break it. Leave the raft in the soup pot and allow any of the clarification vegetables that got into the strainer to drip completely. The consommé will be perfectly clear. Season it with a little salt, let cool, and refrigerate overnight. Ten minutes before serving, bring the consommé to a boil, add the diced butternut garnish, and simmer for 5 minutes.

8. Make the custard.

9. To serve, turn the custard out of the ramekins. For individual custards, place one in the center of each of 6 heated shallow soup plates. For large custards, cut each of them into 6 pieces and arrange 2 pieces in each plate. Add the chopped scallions to the soup and ladle it into the plates. Place the optional fried ginger on top of the custard. Serve immediately.

SECTION 3

IN SECTION THREE WE OFFER SOME *guidelines* TO HELP YOU APPLY TO YOUR DAILY DIET THE IDEAS PRESENTED IN THIS BOOK. WE PROVIDE A LIST OF *resources* TO HELP REDUCE THE PRESENCE OF PESTICIDES IN YOUR FOOD AND YOUR NEIGHBORHOOD. AND WE INTRODUCE YOU TO YOUR *community* OF LOCAL ORGANIC FARMERS AND TO THE STORES, FARM STANDS, AND MARKETS THAT CARRY THEIR PRODUCTS. WE'VE ALSO INCLUDED ADDITIONAL SOURCES OF *information* ON THE SUBJECT OF LOCAL, SEASONAL, ORGANIC PRODUCE.

con·sum·er

\n.\ a buyer of goods and services who, through purchasing power, helps to shape the local, national, and global landscape

This article is adapted from The Green Food Shopper: An Activist's Guide to Changing the Food System, *by Mothers & Others for a Livable Planet. Inspired by nutritionists Joan Dye Gussow and Katherine L. Clancy, whose seminal article, "Dietary Guidelines for Sustainability," appeared in the* Journal of Nutrition Education, *Mothers & Others created this basic checklist for finding and preparing better food. The* Green Food Shopper *offers a variety of strategies for making a difference with your food dollars. See* Resources

Perhaps the greatest gift you can give yourself, your family, and the planet is to make a few simple changes in your diet—changes so pleasing you'll once again, or perhaps for the first time, experience food's rich flavors and aromas, its relationship to the seasons, and the sensual pleasures of preparing and enjoying the family meal.

Today's modern lifestyle puts a premium on eating quickly. No-muss, no-fuss foods that can be prepared in a few minutes have become synonymous with the American diet. We too often choose foods that are heavily processed and packaged. We forgo nourishment in favor of convenience, and in doing so, we reinforce a network of supply and demand that helps undermine local economies and compromise valued traditions. Our eating habits support a method of agriculture that is ecologically unsound, dangerous to the soil, wasteful of energy, and responsible for leaving harmful chemical residues on our food.

Few of us think about the intimate connection between food and the quality of our lives. Food nourishes our bodies, our souls, and the earth, especially when it is grown in a manner that sustains the productivity of the land, conserves finite resources, and supports life.

EIGHT SIMPLE STEPS TO THE NEW GREEN DIET

As consumers, we can make food choices that not only enhance our own health but also contribute to the protection of our natural resources and the long-term sustainability of the food system. The following guidelines will help make planning your family's diet easier, healthier, and greener.

1. Eat a variety of foods

When you eat a wide variety of foods, you're more likely to meet a broad range of nutritional requirements and satisfy your body's need for a diverse diet. Unfortunately, the foods found in supermarkets do not necessarily reflect true biological diversity, given that so many of those products are made from only a few raw food materials, such as corn, wheat, rice, and potatoes. People today rely on only 20 varieties of plants for 90 percent of their food intake. Instead, why not choose a wider variety of whole foods rather than food novelties whose claims to diversity are based on processing techniques and artificial colors and flavors?

8 Ways to Reduce Your Exposure to Pesticides

1. Buy fruits and vegetables in season; the closer produce was grown to your home, the less likely it is to have been treated with chemicals to keep it pest free during storage and shipping.

2. Thoroughly rinse all fruits and vegetables, but don't use detergents; they may leave behind chemical residues not intended for human consumption. Consider peeling any produce that's heavily waxed; the wax may have been mixed with a fungicide to extend the shelf life of the produce.

3. Consider buying organic produce or growing some of your own.

4. Always trim fat from meat and fish; some pesticides build up in fatty tissue.

5. Ask neighbors to let you know when they plan to spray pesticides in their yard so you can be sure kids and pets are out of harm's way. Stay off for at least 24 hours any lawn that's been treated.

(continued next page)

2. Choose locally produced foods

The average mouthful of food travels about 1,300 miles from farm to factory to warehouse to supermarket to table. Foods from local farms are almost always fresher, tastier, and closer to ripeness. What's more, when you buy local products, you support regional growers and help preserve farming nearer to where you live. And locally grown produce is less likely to be treated with postharvest pesticides than is food that travels great distances.

3. Buy produce in season

Out-of-season produce is amazingly energy intensive. It costs about 435 calories to fly one 5-calorie strawberry from California to New York. Out-of-season produce is also more likely to have come from another country, possibly one with less stringent pesticide regulations. Eating frozen fruits and vegetables, especially those from local producers, is your best option during the winter months. Foods that are grown locally and then frozen retain much more of their nutritional value than those that must travel thousands of miles.

4. Buy organically produced food

Organically grown means that food has been grown in a practical, ecological partnership with nature. Organic food is processed minimally to maintain its integrity and is free of artificial ingredients, preservatives, and irradiation. Organic certification is the public's guarantee that the product has been grown without synthetic chemical inputs and has been handled according to strict procedures.

5. Eat fresh, whole foods with adequate starch and fiber

Whole foods—including fruits, vegetables, grains, legumes (peas and beans), nuts, and seeds—are the healthiest foods we can eat. The National Cancer Institute recommends we each "strive for five" servings of fresh fruits and vegetables a day. The complex carbohydrates and fiber they contain play major roles in protecting against cancer, heart disease, and common digestive ailments.

6. If you use a commercial lawn and landscape maintenance service—and some 13 million Americans do—find out exactly what pesticides are applied and how often. Ask if the company offers alternatives. Also, warn kids to stay away from lawn-treatment trucks and to avoid areas with flags that indicate a lawn, tree, or shrub has recently been sprayed with chemicals.

7. Find out what pest-management practices are used in your office and your child's school. Ask to be notified when chemical pesticides are used, and encourage alternative, nonchemical pest control methods.

8. Find out if drinking water in your area has high pesticide residues. You can ask your water supplier for test results or, if you use a private well, have it tested yourself. Filtration methods that remove pesticides are expensive; encourage local officials to work on eliminating the source of contamination.

From "Pesticides: What You Don't Know Can Hurt You" by Sharlene K. Johnson, Ladies' Home Journal, June 1997.

6. Eat fewer and smaller portions of animal products

Modern meat production requires enormous amounts of grain, water, energy, and land for grazing. It takes about 390 gallons of water to produce a pound of beef. Nearly half the energy consumed by the American agriculture industry goes into livestock production. Cattle and other livestock consume more than 70 percent of the grain produced in the United States and approximately one-third of the world's total grain harvest. Animal agriculture also generates considerable amounts of air and water pollution through runoff of animal wastes and discharge from rendering factories. Pork is considered the most resource-intensive animal product, followed by beef and poultry. Eggs and dairy products are far less resource intensive. Animal products, especially beef, also are a major source of fat in the U.S. diet. Reducing meat consumption and eating lower on the food chain protects against heart disease, cancer, and diabetes. When you do eat animal products, choose organically grown products that have been managed in a more ecologically responsible way.

7. Choose minimally processed and packaged foods

Once food leaves the farm, it is subjected to a variety of processes—including packaging—most of which use fossil energy and result in the removal of naturally occurring nutrients. A typical highly processed and highly advertised food product may contain only 7 percent of the original, primary real food declared on the label. Processing offers no real value to the biological diversity of our diets, especially since refined foods are converted into hundreds of products high in fat, salt, or sugar.

8. Prepare your own meals at home

Cooking from scratch may involve a little more labor and a little more time, but you can be sure you'll save money and resources, especially when you consider that you're not paying someone else to prepare the food, put back nutrients removed in processing, package it in a box or can, ship it across the country, and advertise it on television. By preparing foods yourself, you give yourself and your family healthier, more nutritious foods that start with fresh ingredients. And cooking from scratch can be its own reward: a truly creative outlet that brings pleasure, rejuvenates the family meal, and nourishes our bodies and our souls.

HOW CAN I FOSTER ORGANIC FARMING IN MY STATE?

In New Jersey, organic agriculture is still a grassroots movement. The organic farms in our state are small, family farms whose owners often sell their products directly to the public through farm stands and farmers markets. If you are lucky enough to live near an organic grower or market, you may find an abundance of local organic products. If not, those products may be difficult to find.

Weather, pests, and fluctuating market prices make farming a perilous profession. Organic farming is even riskier because it represents a commitment to farm by a set of rules that limit a farmer's ability to declare war on nature's blights. In order to encourage farmers to farm organically, you as a consumer must make it clear that you are willing to support organic growers. And you must make that commitment a long-term lifestyle choice.

To help build a market for local organically grown foods, talk to your grocery store's produce buyer and local farm stand owner and let them know that you want local organically grown products. You may find resistance to the idea, but persistence is the key. Creating strong demand for organically grown products will not only help open the market for organic growers; it will also filter back to conventional farmers, who may be more willing to risk conversion if they know there is a willing market.

If locally grown organic products are not available in your area, support your local conventional farmer. There is always the chance that a farmer will convert to organic in the future but not if a shopping center replaces the farm.

Work with your local and state governments to help preserve farming—not just farmland—in your community. Let local officials know that working farms that produce food are an asset to your community and that you value access to fresh, locally grown food. Show your support for local organic farming by writing to your state representatives. New Jersey is fortunate to have a state agriculture department that is supportive of organic agriculture. Still, much more can be done to develop grant and loan programs that will encourage organic farming in our state.

Organic farming is perfect for New Jersey—small, environmentally sensitive farms growing diverse crops in the midst of an educated market. A strong organic presence also reflects well on the state's image and creates the opportunity to build a national reputation as the Organic Garden State.

New Jersey is one of the top ten U.S. producers of peaches, cranberries, lettuce, blueberries, spinach, asparagus, bell peppers, cucumbers, sweet corn, cabbage, snap beans, eggplant, escarole/endive, and tomatoes.

THE VALUE OF DIVERSITY

One of the central characteristics of New Jersey is its diversity. Some of the aspects of diversity in the Garden State, such as the hills of the north and the flatlands of the south, will never really change. Other aspects are in great peril: open space has become endangered, transportation is narrowing down to the automobile, and building codes and settlement patterns are discouraging variety and promoting uniform, unremarkable housing developments.

The growing lack of diversity is evidenced by the construction of hundreds of homes with little more tying them together than a road that leads away from the community. A diverse community might, within that collection of homes, feature a town center with shops to meet everyday needs—such as those that offer fresh bread and other foods—and with theaters, parks, and restaurants to serve as meeting places for members of the community. The town could be centrally located and accessible by bicycle and pedestrian walkways as well as roadways for cars and public transportation. The homes might serve a variety of economic needs, such as for residents with lower, middle, and upper incomes; for families and single people; and for the young and old alike. For every development there might be farmland set aside for production of seasonal produce and land designated for the management of waste and recyclable materials.

Each of us who have known the Garden State for a few years can think of aspects we love that are in danger; likewise, certain other aspects that develop well. Rather than lose one to gain another, we as citizens and community members need to support diverse and sustainable development. This means that we need to take part in our communities to make sure not only that we are preserving whatever aspect is valuable to us but also that all aspects of a diversified community receive emphasis.

by Michael Rassweiler
North Slope Farm
Lambertville, New Jersey
NOFA-NJ certified

re·sources

\n.\ 1. contact information for the restaurants that donated recipes to this book 2. ordering information on the publications and programs cited in this book 3. other interesting publications, organizations, and Web sites with information about local, seasonal, organic products

CONTACT INFORMATION FOR THE CONTRIBUTING RESTAURANTS

Across the Street

Seen Lippert
Executive Chef

Rustic Mediterranean and American Food utilizing seasonal ingredients

444 East 91st Street
New York, NY 10128
212-722-4000

Arthur's Landing

Steven Singer
Executive Chef

Eclectic combination of Classic Seafood, Pan-Asian, and Southwestern Cuisine. Menu changes seasonally

At Port Imperial
Pershing Circle
Weehawken, NJ 07087
201-867-0777
www.arthurslanding.com

The Bernards Inn

Edward Stone
Executive Chef

Progressive American Cuisine

27 Mine Brook Road
Bernardsville, NJ 07924
908-766-0002
888-766-0002 (toll free)

Church Street Bistro

David G. Kiser
Chef/Proprietor

New Bistro

11½ Church Street
Lambertville, NJ 08530
609-397-4383

Edibles...Naturally! Cafe & Cooking School

Alice Miller
Chef/Owner

Mediterranean/American with an emphasis on natural ingredients

14 Washington Road
Princeton Junction, NJ 08550
609-936-8200

The Forrestal

Yves Vacheresse
Executive Chef

GRATELLA
Contemporary Tuscan Cuisine

HOMESTATE CAFE
American Regional with an emphasis on New Jersey farm products

100 College Road East
Princeton, NJ 08540
609-452-7800

New World Cafe

Ric Orlando
Executive Chef/Partner

World Cuisine Cafe & Caterers

Zena & Saw Kill Road
Woodstock, NY 12498
914-679-2600
www.newworldhomecooking.com

The Rainbow Room

Waldy Malouf
Chef/Director

Elegant Contemporary American Cuisine

30 Rockefeller Plaza
New York, NY 10112
212-632-5000
www.rainbowroom.com

The Ryland Inn

Craig Shelton
Executive Chef/Proprietor

Regional Modern French

Route 22 West
Whitehouse, NJ 08888
908-534-4011

Union Square Cafe

Michael Romano
Executive Chef/Partner

American with rustic Italian flavor

21 East 16th Street
New York, NY 10003
212-243-4020

White Dog Cafe

Kevin von Klause
Chef/Partner

Contemporary American Cuisine with an emphasis on farm-fresh ingredients

3420 Sansom Street
Philadelphia, PA 19104
215-386-9224
www.whitedog.com

Windows on the World

Michael Lomonaco
Chef/Director

Frederic Kieffer
Private Dining Chef

Contemporary American Cuisine

One World Trade Center
New York, NY 10048
212-524-7000
www.windowsontheworld.com

CONTACT INFORMATION FOR THE CONTRIBUTING AUTHORS AND RELATED ORGANIZATIONS

ORGANIC

Northeast Organic Farming Association–New Jersey (NOFA-NJ)

33 Titus Mill Road
Pennington, NJ 08534
609-737-6848

Donna Batcho
Executive Director

NOFA-NJ was founded in 1985 to promote and support local organic agriculture. It is one of seven NOFA chapters in the Northeast. NOFA-NJ provides organic certification for farmers, handlers, and processors and technical support for organic growers; holds an annual winter conference; publishes a free directory of NOFA-NJ certified farms; and publishes a quarterly newsletter.

J. Howard Garrett's Organic Manual

© 1993 The Summit Publishing Group

This book is an excellent guide to the many products and pests encountered by organic gardeners. Written in a clear, straightforward manner, it deals with both organic gardening and lawn care. Available from local bookstores or by calling the Summit Publishing Group at 817-274-1821.

Our Stolen Future

By Theo Colburn,
   Dianne Dumanoski, and
   John Peterson Myers

Published by Penguin Books

Subtitled *Are We Threatening Our Fertility, Intelligence and Survival?* this book explores the effects of pesticides on the sexual development and reproductive systems of animals and humans.

A Shopper's Guide to Pesticides in Produce

$15 plus $3 shipping

Available from:
Environmental Working Group
Suite 600
1718 Connecticut Avenue, NW
Washington, DC 20009
202-667-6982
www.ewg.org

The Environmental Working Group (EWG) is a leading content provider for public-interest groups and concerned citizens who are campaigning to protect the environment. Areas of special emphasis include the threat posed to infants and children by pesticides and other toxic chemicals; the environmental and economic implications of federal farm programs; drinking water contamination by pesticides and other pollutants; wetlands conservation; budget and appropriations policies affecting the environment; and the impact of campaign contributions on environmental policy.

EWG maintains a comprehensive Web site (www.ewg.org) that features most of the organization's publications and numerous searchable databases.

Nutrition Action Health Letter

$24 per year (10 issues)

Published by the Center for Science in the Public Interest (CSPI). Founded in 1971, the CSPI is an independent nonprofit consumer health group that advocates honest food labeling and advertising, safer food additives, and sustainable agriculture.

For more information, contact:
CSPI
1875 Connecticut Avenue, NW
Washington, DC 20009
www.cspinet.org

LOCAL AND SEASONAL

The Northeast Regional Food Guide

By producing these materials, Jennifer L. Wilkins and the Cornell Cooperative Extension have performed a tremendous service for consumers in the northeastern United States who wish to support their local and regional food producers. *The Northeast Regional Food Guide* was a major source of inspiration for our book and is valuable not only in the scope of the information it contains but also in the simplicity and clarity of its presentation.

The Northeast Regional Food Guide Set consists of the Northeast Regional Poster and Produce List and a set of eight Northeast Regional Food Guide Fact Sheets. This is sold as a set for $8.25. The order code is 399NRFGSET.

The poster and seasonal produce list only can be ordered for $4.50. The order code is 399NRFGP.

A set of the eight fact sheets alone is available for $4.25. The order code is 399NRFGFS.

Order from:
Cornell University Resource
   Center
7–8 Business & Technology Park
Ithaca, NY 14850
Tel: 607-255-7660
Fax: 607-255-9946
dist_center@cce.cornell.edu

For questions about the *Northeast Regional Food Guide*, contact:
Jennifer L. Wilkins, Ph.D., R.D.
Senior Extension Associate
Division of Nutritional
   Sciences, Cornell University
607-255-2142

New Jersey Roadside and Urban Markets Directory

This handy booklet contains a county-by-county listing of New Jersey's roadside farm markets as well as urban farm markets and single-commodity product markets.

Available at no charge from the New Jersey Department of Agriculture. To order, call 609-292-8853.

Farm Market listings also are available at the New Jersey State Department Web site: www.state.nj.us/agriculture/. Click "Public Information," then "Publications," and look for "New Jersey Roadside and Urban Markets Directory."

Stocking Up III
By Carol Hupping and the
    Rodale Press staff
Published by Rodale Press

Putting Food By
By Janet Greene,
    Ruth Hertzberg, and
    Beatrice Vaughan
Published by Viking Penguin

These books are excellent guides to the art of preserving food. The recommended cooking times and temperatures for canning have changed since these books were first published. If you have an old edition, consider buying the latest edition or call your cooperative extension for current time and temperature recommendations.

Cooperative Extension Service

Rutgers University, the U.S. Department of Agriculture, and county governments share in planning and financing Cooperative Extension Service work in New Jersey. Rutgers is headquarters for the staff of specialists who work with county agents. Their specialties include agriculture, canning, cooking, food safety, 4-H youth work, marketing, and community development.

For Cooperative Extension Service offices in New Jersey, check the County Government section of your phone book or contact:

Rutgers Cooperative Extension
Cook College
P.O. Box 231
New Brunswick, NJ 08903
908-932-9306

For Cooperative Extension offices in New York, contact:
Cooperative Extension
Roberts Hall
Cornell University
Ithaca, NY 14853
607-255-2237

For Cooperative Extension offices in Pennsylvania, contact:
Cooperative Extension Service
217 Ag Administration Bldg.
Pennsylvania State University
University Park, PA 16802
814-863-3438

FOOD MILES

The Food Miles Action Pack: A Guide to Thinking Globally and Eating Locally
April 1996, £35

Food Miles Report: The Dangers of Long-Distance Food Transport
October 1994, £10

Available from:
The SAFE Alliance
38 Ebury Street
London SW1W 0LU
England

Payment must be made by international money order in pounds sterling.

The SAFE Alliance is a unique coalition of 32 groups including farmer, organic, environment, consumer, animal welfare, development, and public information organizations. The groups share a common vision of food production that is beneficial to the environment and sensitive to consumer demand and that produces safe and healthy food in a manner supportive of rural life and culture worldwide. The main objectives are to:
- facilitate contact and foster links between groups.
- provide information for the public.

- carry out research to gain understanding of the issues.
- communicate common goals to a wider audience through media, publications, events.
- promote sustainable agriculture through policy advocacy, lobbying, dialogue with policy makers.

SAFE was a founding member of the European Network of Alliances for Sustainable Agriculture and has always sought to establish a consensus on these issues at a European level. It is clear that the need for sustainable policies transgresses national borders and that there is a very real need to plan for agricultural reform across Europe. Given the likely expansion of the European Union further into Central and Eastern Europe over the next decade, SAFE believes that a project developing further alliances of nongovernmental organizations both within and between these regions will be of considerable value and will fit into its core work of promoting sustainable food production through alliance building.

For more information on SAFE, contact Vicki Hird at Tel: 011-44-171-823-5660 Fax: 011-44-171-823-5673 E-mail: safe@gn.apc.org www.gn.apc.org/safe

Circle of Poison: Pesticides and People in a Hungry World
By David Weir and
    Mark Schapiro

Available from:
North America Regional
    Center, Suite 810
Pesticide Action Network
116 New Montgomery
San Francisco, CA 94105
415-541-9140
www.panna.org/panna

Since 1982 the Pesticide Action Network (PAN) has campaigned to replace pesticide use with ecologically sound alternatives. As one of five regional centers worldwide, PAN North America links individuals, researchers, farmers, opinion leaders, businesses, and public-interest organizations in Canada, Mexico, and the United States with over 400 consumer, labor, health, environment, and agriculture groups in more than 60 countries.

Information on the Circle of Poison and the exporting of pesticides is also available from:

Foundation for Advancements in Science and Education
Suite 215
4801 Wilshire Boulevard
Los Angeles, CA 90010
213-937-9911
www.fasenet.org

Since 1981 the Foundation for Advancements in Science and Education (FASE) has produced a broad and unique range of public-interest communications and research. FASE staff and associates conduct research and develop and produce film, print, and multimedia products that fulfill educational and social needs. They also are developing a Web site devoted to the issue of pesticide exports.

RECIPES

Chefs Collaborative 2000
25 First Street
Cambridge, MA 02141
617-621-3000
www.chefnet.com/cc2000

The Chefs Collaborative 2000 is a growing network of over a thousand of America's most influential and well-known chefs, working collectively to advance sustainable food choices. The group's mission is to strengthen the farmer-chef relationship and promote locally raised, seasonally fresh foods in each state's restaurants. Nonchefs also are welcomed as members.

CONSUMER

Green Food Shopper: An Activist's Guide to Changing the Food System
By Mothers & Others for a Livable Planet, 1997. To order, send $15 + $3 postage to:
Mothers & Others
40 West 20th Street
New York, NY 10011

Consumer choice—how we eat and the food we buy—can change the way our food is grown. Consumer demand can bring the products of sustainable agriculture into our markets. Clearly, the demand for such products is there and growing: sales of organic foods have risen more than 23 percent annually for the past five years. Mothers & Others' Shoppers' Campaign for Better Food Choices began to harness this consumer power, increasing access to sustainably grown foods in four target cities.

All too often a shopper wants organic or sustainably grown regional food, but finds it's not offered in local supermarkets. In addition, many neighborhoods throughout the United States lack health food stores specializing in fresh organic or locally produced foods. The Shoppers' Campaign set out to change that.

Conceived of as a partnership between consumers and those who produce and market our food, Mothers & Others launched the Shoppers' Campaign for Better Food Choices in the winter of 1993/94. The goals: to build demand for safe, affordable food grown in an environmentally responsible manner; to open the marketplace, making it more responsive to consumers' interests and need for such foods; and to create market opportunities for regional, sustainably produced food.

In *Green Food Shopper*, Mothers & Others has brought together these and other tools and strategies for building awareness and shaping the local marketplace that were tested during the first three years of the campaign. *Green Food Shopper* is designed to help you in your efforts to secure the foods you want in your community. Need advice on how to talk to your supermarket manager? They've done it, and they can help. Want to start a food-buying club or join a Community Supported Agriculture group? This book will help guide you step by step.

You also can help educate your community about where and how its food is grown and the importance of vibrant, local, ecologic agriculture. Organize a tasting with chefs and farmers or a farm tour with children and the press. The book even includes an aisle-by-aisle green forager's guide to supermarkets.

New York office:
Mothers & Others for a Livable Planet/*The Green Guide*
40 West 20th Street
New York, NY 10011-4211
Tel: 212-242-0010
Fax: 212-242-0545
E-mail: mothers@igc.org
www.mothers.org/mothers

West Coast regional office:
Mothers & Others
870 Market Street, Suite 654
San Francisco, CA 94102
Tel: 415-433-0850
Fax: 415-433-0859
E-mail: motherssf@igc.org

OTHER ORGANIZATIONS

American Farmland Trust
1920 N Street, NW, Suite 400
Washington, DC 20036
202-659-5170
www.farmland.org
info@farmland.org

American Farmland Trust (AFT) is the only national, nonprofit conservation organization dedicated to protecting the nation's strategic agricultural resources. Founded in 1980, AFT works to stop the loss of productive farmland and to promote farming practices that lead to a healthy environment. Its activities include public education, technical assistance, policy research and development, and direct land-protection projects. Basic AFT membership is $20 a year.

AFT provides a variety of professional services for state and local governments and public agencies, private organizations, land trusts, and individual landowners. Services include customized information products and workshops on farmland protection and estate planning; policy research, development, and evaluation; farmland protection program implementation; and conservation real estate consulting.

For membership information or general information about AFT, contact the national office or connect to the home page at www.farmland.org.

Bio-Dynamic Farming & Gardening Association
P.O. Box 550
Kimberton, PA 19442
800-516-7797
www.biodynamics.com

Inaugurated in 1924 by Austrian scientist Rudolf Steiner, biodynamic farming seeks to actively work with the health-giving forces of nature.

The Bio-Dynamic Farming and Gardening Association was formed in the United States in 1938. It is a nonprofit, membership organization and is open to the public. The association has an educational focus and conducts conferences, workshops, and seminars. It also publishes books and a bimonthly journal.

Community Supported Agriculture of North America
P.O. Box 57, Jug End Road
Great Barrington, MA 01230
www.umass.edu/umext/CSA

Visit the Web site to find out about Community Supported Agriculture (CSA) and to locate a CSA farm near you.

Food & Water, Inc.
RR 1, Box 68D
Walden, VT 05873
800-EAT-SAFE

Food & Water, Inc., is a nonprofit education and advocacy organization working for safe food and a clean environment. Individual membership is $25 a year and includes four issues of *Food & Water Journal*.

Garden State Heirloom Seed Society
Joe and Bobbi Cavanaugh
P.O. Box 15, Valley Road
Delaware, NJ 07833
908-475-4861

Information on heirlooms and a catalog of heirloom seeds.

Just Food
625 Broadway, Suite 9C
New York, NY 10012
212-674-8124

Just Food nurtures collaborative projects that support the region's farmers while increasing the availability of healthful, locally grown food to the people of New York, especially those with little or no income.

Midwest Organic Alliance
www.organic.org

Basic information on organics and links to interesting sites.

Pure Food Campaign
860 Highway 61
Little Marais, MN 55614
218-226-4164
www.geocities.com/Athens/1527

The Pure Food Campaign (PFC) is a nonprofit, public-interest organization dedicated to building a healthy, safe, and sustainable system of food production and consumption. PFC serves as a global clearinghouse offering information and grassroots technical assistance to citizen activists and nongovernmental organizations concerned about agriculture, food safety, life-form patenting, and genetic engineering.

Sustainable Farming Connection
www.sunsite.unc.edu/farming-connection

An interactive Web site where farmers and others can find and exchange information about production, marketing, commentary, news, action alerts, and links to other sites.

WEB SITES ON COOKING

Digital Chef
www.digitalchef.com

Cooking ideas, recipes, and links to other sites.

Epicurious Food
www.epicurious.com

Includes feature entitled Find Out What Is Ripe at Your Local Farmers Market.

Gemini & Leo's Recipe Links
www.synapse.net/~gemini/recplink.htm

Links to many recipe and cooking sites.

Star Chefs
www.starchefs.com

Features state-by-state list of farmers markets.

di·rec·to·ry

\n\ 1. a list of NOFA-NJ Certified Organic farms and processors 2. farm stands, co-ops, and retailers in New Jersey, New York, and the Philadelphia area that sell local organic products 3. wholesalers of local organic products 4. farms of 5 or more acres that raise organic products but are not third-party certified

---

The NOFA-NJ Certified Organic farms listed in this directory are certified from September 1, 1997, through August 31, 1998. Certification is done on a yearly basis, and farms must be recertified every year. Growers may be decertified at any time if they violate the organic standards.

Unless otherwise indicated, the retailers in this directory have told us they require organic certification from growers or wholesalers. The variety and amount of local organic produce that each retailer carries vary widely. Be sure to ask specifically for local organically grown products. And let us know of retailers of local organic products that are not included in this list.

INDEX TO NOFA-NJ CERTIFIED ORGANIC FARMS & PROCESSORS

NOFA-NJ CERTIFIED ORGANIC FARMS & PROCESSORS AS WELL AS CO-OPS, FARM STANDS & RETAILERS OF LOCAL ORGANIC PRODUCTS

NEW JERSEY

ATLANTIC COUNTY

DuBois Farm
Jim and Chris DuBois
Route 1, Box 438
329 Harding Highway
Buena, NJ 08310
609-697-9356
Description: NOFA-NJ-certified-organic farm, on-farm seasonal retail, wholesale
Products: most vegetables, water–melon, cantaloupe, strawberries
Open: call for hours and times

BERGEN COUNTY

Fresh Organics
888-9FRESH9
www.freshorganics.com
Description: home delivery of organic produce

Kings Super Markets
70 Union Avenue
Cresskill, NJ 07626
201-541-4900

112-130 Linwood Plaza
Fort Lee, NJ 07024
201-363-4912

381 Washington Avenue
Hillsdale, NJ 07642
201-722-4690

112 North Maple Avenue
Ridgewood, NJ 07450
201-493-4924

Description: supermarkets

Natural Selection
357 Fairview Avenue
Fairview, NJ 07022
201-945-7200
Description: natural foods store
Open: T, W, F, Sat 9am–6pm, M, Th 9am–7pm

Old Hook Farm
Bruce and Mary Marek
650 Old Hook Road
Emerson, NJ 07630
201-265-4835

Description: NOFA-NJ-certified-organic farm, on-farm year-round retail store, farmers market participant
Products: fresh produce, frozen/refrigerated/dried fruit, nuts, beans, grains, vegetable plants, herbs, houseplants, dairy products
Open: T–Sat 9am–6pm, Sun 9am–4pm

Surrey International Natural Foods
33 Ridge Road
North Arlington, NJ 07032
201-991-1905
Description: natural foods store
Open: M–F 9am–8pm, Sat 9am–6pm, Sun 9am–3pm

Tony Di Pippo's Farm
Linda Di Pippo
148 Crescent Avenue
Waldwick, NJ 07463
201-445-4984
Description: NOFA-NJ-certified-organic farm with on-farm seasonal retail stand, CSA, farmers market participant
Products: herbs, vegetables from spring greens to fall potatoes
Open: July–October

Whole Foods Market
Ridgewood Plaza
44 Godwin Place
Ridgewood, NJ 07450
Description: natural foods super-market
Opening in 1998

BURLINGTON COUNTY

Garden of Eden Natural Foods
Ramblewood Center
1155 North Route 73
Mt. Laurel, NJ 08054
609-778-1971
Description: natural foods store
Open: M–F 10am–9pm, Sat 10am–6pm, Sun 10am–3pm

Mill Creek Organic Farm
Ken and Nancy Muckenfuss
105A Eayrestown Road
Medford, NJ 08055
609-953-0372
Description: NOFA-NJ-certified-organic farm, CSA, on-farm seasonal retail, wholesale
Products: vegetables, beef, eggs, strawberries, corn, soybeans, rye, hay, straw, wheat, chicken feed

Open: June through October; call ahead for store hours

Whole Foods Market
Greentree Square
940 Route 73 North
Marlton, NJ 08053
Description: natural foods supermarket
Opening in 1998

Zagara's
Town Place at Marlton
Route 73 and Brick Road
Marlton, NJ 08053
609-983-5700
Description: natural foods store
Open: M–F 9am–9pm, Sat 8am–9pm, Sun 8am–8pm

CAMDEN COUNTY

Iuliucci Farms
Steve Iuliucci
141 Route 73 South, RD5
Braddock, NJ 08037
609-567-4186
Description: NOFA-NJ-certified-organic farm, wholesale, direct sales
Products: soybeans, wheat, rye, corn

Winslow Farms Conservancy
Anthony Sacco
P.O. Box 196
Winslow, NJ 08095-0196
609-561-0628
Description: NOFA-NJ-certified-organic farm
Products: hay, grain, vegetables

CAPE MAY COUNTY

J. C. Hazlett Farm & Market
Jim C. Hazlett
570 Route 47 North
Cape May Court House, NJ 08210
609-861-5551
Description: NOFA-NJ-certified-organic farm, wholesale, direct sales
Products: vegetables, herbs, hay

CUMBERLAND COUNTY

DuBose Farm
Syvella DuBose
28 Ayers Lane
Bridgeton, NJ 08302
609-455-5811
Description: NOFA-NJ-certified-organic farm, farmers market

participant, direct to health food stores and restaurants

Products: okra, corn, string beans, lima beans, peas, herbs, and crafted herbal products

ESSEX COUNTY

Clairmont Health Food Center

515 Bloomfield Avenue
Montclair, NJ 07042
973-744-7122
Description: natural foods store
Open: M–Sun 8am–10pm

Fresh Fields/Whole Foods

187 Millburn Avenue
Millburn, NJ 07041
973-376-4668

701 Bloomfield Avenue
Montclair, NJ 07042
973-746-5110
Description: natural foods super-market selling local organic produce in season including Garden State Organic Growers Cooperative tomatoes (1997 growing season)

Kings Super Markets

393 Main Street
Chatham, NJ 07928
973-635-4400

255 South Livingston Avenue
Livingston, NJ 07039
973-535-4940

159 Maplewood Avenue
Maplewood, NJ 07040
973-761-4092

784 Springfield Avenue
Summit, NJ 07901
908-598-4500

650 Valley Road
Upper Montclair, NJ 07043
973-509-4828

300 Pompton Avenue
Verona, NJ 07044
973-571-4188

Point View Shopping Center
201 Berdan Avenue
Wayne, NJ 07470
973-872-4140

875 Bloomfield Avenue
West Caldwell, NJ 07006
973-244-4540

Description: supermarkets

Purple Dragon Co-op

165 Willow Street
Bloomfield, NJ 07003
973-429-0391
Description: home delivery of certified-organic produce

HUDSON COUNTY

Hoboken Farmboy

229 Washington Street
Hoboken, NJ 07030
201-656-0581
Description: natural foods store
Open: M–Sat 8am–10pm, Sun 8am–9pm

Jersey City Farmboy

82 Hawthorne Street
Jersey City, NJ 07301
201-963-9281
Description: natural foods store
Open: M–Sat 9am–7pm

John's Natural Foods

486 Broadway
Bayonne, NJ 07002
201-858-0088
Description: natural foods store
Open: M, Th, F 9:30am–9pm, T, W, Sat 9:30am–6pm, Sun 10am–5pm

NOFA-NJ/Garden State Organic Growers Cooperative Farmers Market

NY Waterway at Arthur's Landing Restaurant
Pershing Circle
Weehawken, NJ 07087
Description: region's only certified-organic farmers market
Open: Fridays from 3:30 to 7:30pm during the 1997 growing season. For 1998, call NOFA-NJ at 609-737-6848.

HUNTERDON COUNTY

Amwell Valley Organic Grains

Debbi and Steve Spayd
P.O. Box 411
Ringoes, NJ 08551
609-397-4583
Description: NOFA-NJ-certified-organic processor with mail-order business; call for brochure and order form
Products: popcorn–microwave, bagged, and gift jars, whole wheat flour–stone-ground fresh, sunflower seeds

Basil Bandwagon

202 Route 31 South
Ringoes, NJ 08551
908-788-5737
Description: natural foods store
Open: M–Th 10am–8pm, F 9am–8pm, Sat 9am–6pm, Sun 11am–5pm

Honey Moon Botanicals

Beth Lambert
56 Farmersville Road
Califon, NJ 07830
908-832-5725
Description: NOFA-NJ-certified-organic farm, contract wholesale
Products: medicinal herbs: motherwort, figwort, lemon balm, horehound, hyssop, etc.

Kings Super Markets

450 Route 206N & Hills Drive
Bedminster, NJ 07921
908-719-4960

100 Morristown Road
Bernardsville, NJ 07924
908-204-4840

Rts. 523 and 22
White House Station, NJ 08889
908-470-4022
Description: supermarkets

New Horizon Plant Farm

Tony Sampaio
555 Charlestown Road
Hampton, NJ 08827
908-735-7337
Description: NOFA-NJ-certified-organic retail greenhouse
Products: organic herb and organic vegetable plants and bedding plants, flowering plants and ground covers

North Slope Farm

Michael Rassweiler and Julia Ritter
1201 Linvale-Harbourton Road
Lambertville, NJ 08530
609-466-4191
Description: NOFA-NJ-certified-organic farm with on-farm seasonal retail stand, CSA, farmers market participant, direct sales to restaurants
Products: 70 varieties of vegetables, herbs, flowers, and some seasonal fruit. Dry goods, natural foods, and heirloom vegetables. Educational and farm visits
Open: June to November, W–Sat 10am–7pm, educational program and farm visits by appointment

MERCER COUNTY

Coventry Farm
Kathy Winnant
549 Great Road
Princeton, NJ 08540
609-924-7643
Description: NOFA-NJ-certified-organic farm with seasonal farm stand and wholesale
Products: greens, vegetables, cut flowers
Open: June through October, Sat–Sun 10–2; call ahead to be sure store is open

Kokoro Gardens
John and Yukiko Johnson
377 Walnut Lane
Princeton, NJ 08540
609-683-4208
Farm located in Pennington, NJ
Description: NOFA-NJ-certified-organic farm, wholesale, direct sales and CSA
Products: salad greens, herbs, vegetables, and strawberries

McCaffrey's
301 North Harrison Street
Princeton, NJ 08540
609-683-1600
Open: M–Sat 8am–10pm, Sun 8am–8pm

Route 571 & Southfield Road
West Windsor, NJ 08512
609-799-3555
Open: M–Sat 7am–10pm, Sun 8am–8pm
Description: supermarkets, some local organic produce in season

Nassau Street Seafood
256 Nassau Street
Princeton, NJ 08540
609-921-0620
Description: seafood/produce store, certification not required
Open: M–F 9am–7pm, Sat 9am–6pm, Sun 9am–3pm

Watershed Organic Farm
Jim Kinsel
260 Wargo Road
Pennington, NJ 08534
609-737-8899
609-737-8590 (fax)
Description: NOFA-NJ-certified-organic farm, region's largest seasonal CSA (no on-farm retail), farmers market participant, direct to restaurants, wholesale

Products: seasonal vegetables: arugula to zucchini; strawberries and melons

Whole Earth Center
360 Nassau Street
Princeton, NJ 08540
609-924-7429
Description: Princeton area's oldest and most complete natural foods store, founded in 1970, offers natural and organically grown foods, fresh whole-grain baked goods, prepared foods from its gourmet vegetarian deli, full range of local organic produce, organically grown potted herbs, and vegetable transplants for gardens in season
Open: M–F 10–7, Sat 10–6

MIDDLESEX COUNTY

E. R. & Son Farm
Ed and Rose Lidzbarski
572 Buckelew Avenue
Jamesburg, NJ 08831
732-521-2591 (phone/fax)
Description: NOFA-NJ-certified-organic farm with on-farm store open year-round, wholesale
Products: vegetables and fruit; in addition to its own seasonal organic produce, offers dry goods, dairy products, and honey
Open: W–F 10am–6pm, Sat–Sun 10am–5pm

George Street Coop
89 Morris Street
New Brunswick, NJ 08901
732-247-8280
Description: natural foods store
Open: M–F 10am–8pm, Sat 10am–6pm, Sun 11am–6pm

MONMOUTH COUNTY

Healthfair
625 Branch Avenue
Little Silver, NJ 07739
732-747-3140
Description: natural foods store
Open: M, W, Sat 9am–6pm, Th, F 9am–7pm, Sun 9am–5pm

Merrick Farm
Susan Keymer & Juan George
98 Merrick Road
Farmingdale, NJ 07727
732-938-2491
Description: NOFA-NJ-certified-organic farm
Products: vegetables, herbs, and berries

Pauline's Health Food
3585 Route 9 North
Freehold, NJ 07728
732-303-0854
Open: M–F 9:30am–7pm, Sat 9:30am–6pm, Sun 11am–5pm

303 Route 9 South
Manalapan, NJ 07726
732-308-0449
Open: M–Th 9:30am–8:30pm, F 9:30am–8pm, Sat 9:30am–6pm, Sun 11am–5pm

Description: natural foods stores

River Bend Farm
Susan and Michael Marchese
200 Casino Drive
Farmingdale, NJ 07727
732-938-5137
Description: NOFA-NJ-certified-organic farm
Products: vegetables

Second Nature
65 Broad Street
Red Bank, NJ 07701
732-747-6448
www.monmouth.com/~secondnature
Description: natural and organic foods and products, emphasis on local organic produce in season during the growing season, 50–60% of produce is local organic
Open: M–F 10am–8pm, Sat 10am–6pm, Sun 10am–5pm

Side Road Gardens
Mary Ann Cavallaro
P.O. Box 2376
Princeton, NJ 08543-2376
609-984-7874
Farm in Holmdel, NJ
Description: NOFA-NJ-certified-organic farm
Products: medicinal herbs

MORRIS COUNTY

Health Shoppe

Chester Spring Shopping Center
Route 206
Chester, NJ 07930
908-879-7555

66 Morris Street
Morristown, NJ 07960
973-538-9131

Troy Hills Shopping Center
1123 Route 46 East
Parsippany, NJ 07054
973-263-8348
Description: natural foods store
with 3 locations
Open: M–F 9am–9pm,
Sat 9am–7pm, Sun 9am–6pm

Kariba Farms

Dr. Martin Welt
14 Ridgedale Avenue
Cedar Knolls, NJ 07927
973-292-3600
Description: NOFA-NJ-certified-
organic wholesale handler/
processor
Products: dried vegetables, dried
herbs, and dried fruit

Kings Super Markets

86 East Main Street
Mendham, NJ 07945
973-543-4493

191 South Street
Morristown, NJ 07960
973-898-4512
Description: supermarkets

Mrs. Erb's Good Food

20 First Avenue
Denville, NJ 07834
973-627-5440
Description: 4,000-square-foot, full-
service, natural gourmet foods
store that has specialized in
organically grown produce and
foods since 1986; deli uses almost
only organic ingredients; 100% of
produce is local organic in season
Open: M–F 9am–8pm,
Sat 9am–7pm, Sun 10am–5pm

Vallevue of Morristown

Tom Pote
P.O. Box 231
Chester, NJ 07930
908-879-2269
Farm is in Morristown, NJ
Description: NOFA-NJ-certified-
organic farm, wholesale, CSA
Products: vegetables

OCEAN COUNTY

Earth Goods

777 East Bay Avenue
Manahawkin, NJ 08050
609-597-7744
Description: natural and organic
whole foods ranging from whole
organic grains to foods for those
with special dietary needs;
approximately 25% of produce is
local organic in season
Open: M–F 10am–7pm,
Sat 10am–6pm, Sun 11am–4pm

Natural Foods General Store

675 Batchelor Street
Toms River, NJ 08753
732-240-0024
Description: natural foods store,
certification not required
Open: M–F 10am–6pm,
W 10am–8pm, Sat 10am–5pm,
Sun 12pm–5pm

Stone Hollow Farm

George and Emily McNulty
136 Route 72
Barnegat, NJ 08005
609-698-2405 (phone/fax)
Description: NOFA-NJ-certified-
organic farm, CSA, retail,
wholesale
Products: wide variety of herbs,
vegetables, berries, Asian pears,
and dried tomatoes, organically
raised calves

PASSAIC COUNTY

Jerry's in the Park

200 Main Avenue
Passaic Park, NJ 07055
973-473-6645
Description: produce store
Open: M–W 7:30am–7:30pm,
Th 7:30am–9pm,
F 7:30–sundown, Sun 8am–5pm

SALEM COUNTY

Neptune Farm

Torrey Reade and Dick
McDermott
723 Harmersville-Canton Road
Salem, NJ 08079
609-935-3612
Description: NOFA-NJ-certified-
organic farm, mostly wholesale
Products: asparagus, blueberries,
squash, leeks, watermelon,

broccoli, tomatoes, peppers,
potatoes, other vegetables; beef,
lamb, pork, eggs, hay, grain, wool,
custom growing

SOMERSET COUNTY

Carriage Farm

Edward and Susan Clerico
2 Clerico Lane, Box 1079
Belle Mead, NJ 08502
908-369-6989
Description: NOFA-NJ-certified-
organic farm
Products: vegetables and hay

Farmer John's Organic Produce

Mark Canright
31 King George Road
Warren, NJ 07059
732-356-9498 (phone/fax)
Description: NOFA-NJ-certified-
organic farm with year-round
farm stand and retail store
Products: fruit, vegetables, dry
goods, dairy, meat, flowers
Open: Th 10am–7pm,
Sat 10am–6pm

Fountain of Vitality

32 Route 206 South
Belle Mead, NJ 08502
908-874-3866

368B Springfield Avenue
Berkeley Heights, NJ 07922
908-464-3370

650 Shunpike Road
Chatham, NJ 07928
973-377-8663

100 Mountain Boulevard
Warren, NJ 07060
732-469-0088
Description: natural foods store,
certification not required
Open: M–Sat 10am–6pm,
Th 10am–8pm, Sun 11am–4pm

Kings Super Markets

64 Mountain Blvd.
Warren, NJ 07059
908-226-4988
Description: supermarket

SUSSEX COUNTY

Catalpa Ridge Farm
Rick Sisti
P.O. Box 257
Newfoundland, NJ 07435
973-209-4903
Farm is in Wantage, NJ
Description: NOFA-NJ-certified-
organic farm, CSA only
Products: vegetables, fruits, hay

Fair Acres Farm
Richard Kaweske
1343 Route 23
Wantage, NJ 07461-3607
973-875-7718
Description: NOFA-NJ-certified-
organic farm
Products: vegetables, hay

Fields of Dreams
Norbert Hufnagl
117 Fredon-Springdale Road
Newton, NJ 07860
973-300-0563
973-300-0595 (fax)
Description: NOFA-NJ-certified-
organic farm, farmers market
participant, chefs, contract,
delivery from northern New
Jersey to New York, processor,
restaurant, wholesale
Products: vegetables, flowers, herbs,
heirloom, specialty varieties
Open: by appointment only

Maple Farm
Scott Steinetz
19 Northridge Road
Denville, NJ 07834
973-328-3999
Farm is in Wantage, NJ
Description: NOFA-NJ-certified-
organic farm, wholesale only
Products: greens, peppers, onions,
garlic, potatoes, tomatoes,
shallots, hay, etc.

Seed 'N Sprout
281 Route 94
Vernon, NJ 07462
973-209-8555
Description: natural foods store
selling local organic produce
Open: M–Th 10am–6pm,
F 10am–8pm, Sat 10am–5pm,
Sunday 11am–5pm

Stephens Farm
Ted Stephens
467 Route 284
Sussex, NJ 07461
973-875-2849

Description: NOFA-NJ-certified-
organic farm, seasonal on-farm
retail, wholesale, farmers market
participant
Products: vegetables, fruits/berries,
hay and feed grain, herbs
Open: mid-May through October,
W–Sun 9am–7pm

Sussex County Food Co-op
30 Moran Street
Newton, NJ 07860
973-579-1882
Description: co-op that buys from
local organic growers, certification not required
Open: M–Th, Sat 9:30am–5:30pm,
F 9:30am–9pm, Sun 1:15pm–5pm

Upper Meadows Farm
Leonard Pollara
6 Pollara Lane
Montague, NJ 07827
973-293-7350
Description: NOFA-NJ-certified-
organic farm, wholesale, retail by
appointment
Products: seasonal vegetables, grain
(oats, wheat, barley), hay, eggs,
chicken, pork, beef

Walnut Grove Farm
Les and Deb Guile
189 Route 519
Augusta, NJ 07822
973-383-5029
Description: NOFA-NJ-certified-
organic farm, on-farm retail
Products: all vegetables (except
asparagus), herbs, garlic
Open: mid-May through October,
W–Sun 9am–7pm

UNION COUNTY

Autumn Harvest Natural Foods
1625 East 2nd Street
Scotch Plains, NJ 07076
908-322-2130
Description: natural foods store
Open: M, F 9:30am–6:30pm,
T–Th 9:30am–7:30pm,
Sat 9:30am–5:30pm;
call for Sunday hours

D'Artagnan
280 Wilson Avenue
Newark, NJ 07105
800-327-8246
Description: retail mail-order/
wholesale distributor of fresh
game and organic chickens and
turkeys

Kings Super Markets
434 Springfield Avenue
Berkeley Heights, NJ 07922
908-464-4476

300 South Avenue
Garwood, NJ 07027
908-518-4360

778 Morris Turnpike
Short Hills, NJ 07078
973-258-4000

Description: supermarkets

WARREN COUNTY

Asbury's Natural Village Farm
Louise Bruno
P.O. Box 165
Asbury-Bloomsbury Road and
Main Street
Asbury, NJ 08802
908-638-8079
Description: NOFA-NJ-certified-
organic farm, CSA, farmers
market participant, direct to
restaurants and stores
Products: vegetables, flowers, herbs

Fiddler's Farm
Dick Moran and Donald Sharp
4 Old Orchard Road
Hardwick, NJ 07825
908-362-7595
Farm is in Stillwater, NJ
Description: NOFA-NJ-certified-
organic farm, on-farm retail,
farmers market participant
Products: vegetables

Heirloom Harvest Farm
David Size
32 Pippin Hill Road
Blairstown, NJ 07825
908-362-9046
Description: NOFA-NJ-certified-
organic farm
Products: heirloom vegetables,
antique apples, mushrooms,
herbs, heirloom seed production

Starbrite Farm
Dick Moran
4 Old Orchard Road
Hardwick, NJ 07825
908-362-7595
Description: NOFA-NJ-certified-
organic farm, farmers market
participant, direct sales,
wholesale
Products: vegetables, herbs, berries

NEW YORK

COLUMBIA COUNTY

Hawthorne Valley Farm
327 Route 21C
Ghent, NY 12075
518-672-4465
Description: CSA farm, sell year-round at Union Square Farmers Market in New York on Wednesday and Sunday; Hawthorne Valley Dairy makes yogurt, raw-milk cheese, and quark; raw milk sold in the farm store, as are its other products

KINGS COUNTY

Urban Organic
230 7th Street
Brooklyn, NY 11215
718-499-4321
Description: home delivery subscription service, includes local organic produce

MANHATTAN

Agata & Valentina
1505 First Avenue (at 79th Street)
New York, NY 10021
212-452-0690
Description: Italian specialty foods store
Open: M–Sun 8am–9pm

Dean & Deluca
560 Broadway
New York, NY 10012
212-226-6800
Description: gourmet foods store selling local organic vegetables, certification not required
Open: M–Sat 10am–8pm,
   Sun 10am–7pm

Gourmet Garage
Corner Broome and Mercer
New York, NY
212-941-5850
Open: M–Sun 7:30am–9pm

301 East 64th Street
New York, NY
212-535-5880
Open: M–Sun 7:30am–8:30pm

2567 Broadway
New York, NY
212-663-0656
Open: M–Sun 7:30am–9pm
Description: gourmet foods stores

Gramercy Natural Food Center
427 Second Avenue
New York, NY 10010
212-725-1651
Description: natural foods store
Open: M–F 10am–8pm,
   Sat 10am–6pm, Sun 12pm–5pm

Integral Yoga Natural Foods
229 West 13th Street
New York, NY 10011
212-243-2642
Description: natural foods store
Open: M–F 10am–9:30pm,
   Sat 10am–8:30pm,
   Sun 12pm–6:30pm

Jefferson Market
450 Avenue of the Americas
New York, NY 10011
212-533-3377
Description: gourmet foods store
Open: M–Fri 7:30am–9pm,
   Sat 8am–8pm, Sun 9am–8pm

LifeThyme
410 Sixth Avenue
New York, NY 10011
212-420-9099
Description: natural foods store
Open: M–F 8am–10pm,
   Sat–Sun 9am–10pm

Mayfair
166 Second Avenue (at 10th Street)
New York, NY 10003
212-475-2828
Description: natural foods store; nearly half the store is devoted to organic food
Open: M–Sat 7am–11pm,
   Sun 8am–11pm

Prana Foods
125 First Avenue
New York, NY 10003
212-982-7306
Description: natural foods store
Open: M–Sat 9am–9pm,
   Sun 10am–7pm

Soho Provisions
518 Broadway
New York, NY 10012
212-334-4311
Description: gourmet foods store
Open: M–Sun 10am–8pm

Super Natural
728 Ninth Avenue
New York, NY 10019
212-399-9200
Description: natural foods store
Open: M–F 8am–8:30pm,
   Sat 9am–7pm, Sun 10am–6pm

Urban Roots
51 Avenue A
New York, NY 10009
212-780-0288
Description: natural foods store
Open: M–Sun 9am–10pm

The Vinegar Factory
431 East 91st Street, between 1st and York Avenues
New York, NY 10128
212-987-0885
Description: market-concept retail store with organic produce department, organic breads from Eli's Bread, very large prepared food section, strong commitment to quality; buys from the Garden State Organic Growers Cooperative in season
Open: M–Sun 7am–9pm

Whole Foods
2421 Broadway
New York, NY 10024
212-874-4000
Open: M–Sun 8am–11pm

117 Prince Street
New York, NY 10012
212-982-1000
Open: M–F 8am–10pm,
   Sat–Sun 9am–10pm
Description: natural foods stores

NEW YORK CITY GREENMARKETS

All markets are open 8am–6pm unless otherwise noted. Several organic growers sell at these markets. For more information, call the Greenmarket office at 212-477-3220.

Abingdon Square
West 12th St. & Eighth Ave.
Open: May through December,
   Sat 8am–3 pm

Bowling Green
Broadway & Battery Place
Open: year-round, Thursday

City Hall
Chambers & Centre Streets
Open: year-round, Tuesday and
   Friday 8am–3pm

Federal Plaza
Broadway & Thomas Streets
Open: year-round, Friday

Lafayette Street
Lafayette & Spring Streets
Open: July through November,
   Thursday

Minisink Townhouse
West 143rd St. & Lenox Ave.
Open: mid-July through October,
  Tuesday

P.S. 44
West 77th St. & Columbus Ave.
Open: year-round, Sun 10am–5pm

P.S. 234
Greenwich & Chamber Streets,
  south corner
Open: April through December,
  Saturday

Sheffield Plaza
West 57th St. & Ninth Ave.
Open: year round, Wednesday and
  Saturday

St. Mark's Church
East 10th St. & Second Ave.
Open: June through November,
  Tuesday

Tompkins Square
7th Street & Avenue A
Open: year round, Sunday

Union Square
East 17th Street & Broadway
Open: year round, Monday,
  Wednesday, Friday, Saturday

Verdi Square
West 72nd Street & Broadway
Open: mid-June through
  November, Saturday

Washington Market Park
Greenwich & Chamber Streets,
  north corner
Open: June through December,
  Wednesday

West 97th Street
Between Amsterdam & Columbus
  Avenues
Open: June through December,
  Friday 8am–3pm

West 175th Street
Broadway
Open: June through December,
  Thursday

World Trade Center
Church & Fulton Streets
Open: June through November,
  Tuesday; year-round, Thursday

BRONX GREENMARKETS

Lincoln Hospital
East 149th St. & Park Ave.
Open: mid-July through October,
  Tuesday and Friday

Poe Park
East 192nd Street & Grand
  Concourse
Open: mid-July through November,
  Tuesday 8am–3pm

BROOKLYN
GREENMARKETS

Albee Square
Fulton St. & DeKalb Ave.
Open: mid-July through October,
  Wednesday 8am–3pm

Borough Hall
Court & Remsen Streets
Open: year-round, Tuesday and
  Saturday

Grand Army Plaza
At entrance to Prospect Park
Open: year-round, Saturday

Williamsburg
Havemeyer & Broadway
Open: mid-July through October,
  Thursday

Windsor Terrace
At entrance to Prospect Park at
  Bartell Pritchard Square
Open: July through November,
  Wednesday

STATEN ISLAND
GREENMARKETS

St. George
Borough Hall Parking Lot
St. Mark's & Hyatt Streets
Open: mid-June through
  November, Saturday

PENNSYLVANIA

ADAMS COUNTY

Organic Emerald Farm
Maria Medici and Jerry Maloney
744 Harney Road
Littlestown, PA 17340-9359
717-359-0412
Description: NOFA-NJ-certified-
  organic farm, seasonal on-farm
  retail, health food store, farmers
  market participant
Products: vegetables, grains, hay

BERKS COUNTY

Burkholder's Farm
Aaron Burkholder
460 Bowers Road
Kutztown, PA 19530
610-682-7460

Description: NOFA-NJ-certified-
  organic farm, wholesale only
Products: vegetables

**Cornerstone Grain
Processing**
Mel Gelsinger
RD 1, Box 378
Robesonia, PA 19551
610-693-5529
Description: NOFA-NJ-certified-
  organic wholesale grain processor
Products: custom livestock feed
  blends

Rodale Institute Farm
Jeff Moyer
611 Siegfriedale Road
Kutztown, PA 19530-9749
610-683-1420
Description: NOFA-NJ-certified-
  organic farm, seasonal on-farm
  retail stand, wholesale, direct to
  restaurants and stores
Products: vegetables, grains, bedding
  plants, cut flowers, compost
Open: call for hours

BUCKS COUNTY

Branch Creek Farm
Mark and Judy Dornstreich
1501 Branch Road
Perkasie, PA 18944
215-257-8491
Description: NOFA-NJ-certified-
  organic farm, year-round direct
  sales to restaurants
Products: vegetables, herbs, salad
  greens

Eden Farm
Lois Dribin
5613 Point Pleasant Pike
Doylestown, PA 18901
215-297-0203
Description: NOFA-NJ-certified-
  organic farm, wholesale only
Products: vegetables

Franklin Farm
John and Linda Franklin
2535 Township Road
Quakertown, PA 18951
610-346-8107
Description: NOFA-NJ-certified-
  organic farm, seasonal on-farm
  retail stand, direct to restaurants
Products: vegetables, herbs, hay
Open: call ahead for days and hours

Genuardi's Family Markets
900 Neshaminy Mall
Bensalem, PA 19020
215-357-1340

4275 County Line Road
Chalfont, PA 18914
215-997-2883

73 Old Dublin Pike
Doylestown, PA 18901
215-345-1830

168 North Flowers Mill Road
Langhorne, PA 19047
215-741-3360

2890 South Eagle Road
Newtown, PA 18940
215-579-1310

Description: supermarkets

NBA Organic Food Co-Op
329 Otter Street
Bristol, PA 19007
215-781-6303
Description: natural foods store that
stocks only organically grown
products, home delivery available
Open: W–F 10am–6:30pm,
Sat 10am–4:30pm

New Hope Natural Market
415B Old York Road
New Hope, PA 18938
215-862-3441
Description: natural foods store,
certification not required
Open: M–F 10am–7pm,
Sat 10am–6pm, Sun 12pm–6pm

The Salad Garden
Sheila McDuffie
527 Center Hill Road
Upper Black Eddy, PA 18972
610-847-2853
Description: NOFA-NJ-certified-
organic farm, on-farm retail store
open year-round
Products: organic vegetables and
fruits, milk, cheese, bread, free-
range eggs, honey, herbs, vinegars,
preserves, candles, herbal
cosmetics, flowers, books, herb
plants, potpourri
Open: F–Sun 10am–6 pm

The Sproutman
Murray Tizer
Box 308
Upper Black Eddy, PA 18972
610-982-9108
Description: NOFA-NJ-certified-
organic farm, wholesale only
Products: 16 varieties of certified
organic sprouts

CHESTER COUNTY

C. P. Yeatman & Sons, Inc.
Tim Hihn
600 Baker Station Road
West Grove, PA 19390
610-869-3595
Description: NOFA-NJ-certified-
organic farm, on-farm retail store
featuring certified organic mushrooms, wholesale, distributor
Products: mushrooms
Open: M–F 10am–5pm, Sat 10am–
4pm, Sun 12–4pm, call to verify

Fresh Fields
821 Lancaster Avenue
Wayne, PA 19087
610-688-9400
Description: natural foods
supermarket
Open: M–Sat 8am–9pm,
Sun 8am–8pm

Genuardi's Family Markets
1039 Route 113
Phoenixville, PA 19460
610-935-2688

500 Chesterbrook Boulevard
Wayne, PA 19087
610-296-4420

1570 Paoli Pike
West Chester, PA 19380
610-344-0040

Description: supermarkets

Payne Mushroom Farm
John Payne
P.O. Box 275
Nottingham, PA 19362
610-932-3180
Description: NOFA-NJ-certified-
organic farm, wholesale only
Products: shiitake mushrooms

Strictly Organic Inc.
Al Wolgemuth
34 Evergreen Road
Lebanon, PA 17042
717-273-1555
Mill is in Atglen, PA
Description: NOFA-NJ-certified-
organic wholesale grain processor
Products: complete feeds,
concentrates, ingredients for
organic feeds

DELAWARE COUNTY

Genuardi's Family Markets
475 Glen Eagle Square
Glen Mills, PA 19342
610-558-3160

4855 West Chester Pike
Newtown Square, PA 19073
610-325-7200

550 East Lancaster Avenue
St. Davids, PA 19087
610-989-0781

950 Baltimore Pike
Springfield, PA 19064
610-604-1570

Description: supermarkets

FRANKLIN COUNTY

Diller Farm
J. Arnold Diller
8194 Helman Road
Waynesboro, PA 17268
717-762-5593
Description: NOFA-NJ-certified-
organic farm, wholesale only
Products: dairy, field crops

Highland Acres
Bonnie Wilson
22135 Path Valley Road
Doylesburg, PA 17219
717-349-2113
Description: NOFA-NJ-certified-
organic farm, seasonal on-farm
retail store, Tuscarora Organic
Growers Co-op and farmers
market participant
Products: melons, potatoes, cabbage,
chard, mint, turnips, garlic,
rhubarb, strawberries, eggplant,
tomatillos, tomatoes, fingerlings
Open: call ahead for hours

Olde Deep Well Farm Trust
R. William Dunmire
1583 Two Turn Road
Shippensburg, PA 17257
717-532-3621
Description: NOFA-NJ-certified-
organic farm, wholesale only
Products: field crops, hay

FULTON COUNTY

Donald Lake Farm
Donald Lake
HCR 80, Box 228
Big Cove Tannery, PA 17212
717-573-2823
Description: NOFA-NJ-certified-
organic farm, Tuscarora Organic
Growers Co-op
Products: strawberries, shiitake
mushrooms, asparagus

LANCASTER COUNTY

Eberly
1095 Mount Airy Road
Stevens, PA 17578
717-336-6440
Description: natural and organic
poultry wholesaler/retailer
offering organic chickens and
turkeys and free-range ducks,
geese, and capons.

McGeary Grain Inc.
David Poorbaugh
P.O. Box 299
Lancaster, PA 17608
717-394-6843
Description: NOFA-NJ-certified-
organic wholesale grain handler
Products: corn, soybeans, wheat

Simple Gifts Farm
Sam and Katy Reist
2121 River Road
Washington Boro, PA 17582
717-684-5210
Description: NOFA-NJ-certified-
organic farm, seasonal on-farm
retail store, CSA, wholesale
Products: vegetables
Open: call ahead for hours

Sunsprout of Lancaster Co.
Jere and Pamela Hull
526 North Charlotte Street
Lancaster, PA 17603
717-392-2707
Description: NOFA-NJ-certified-
organic farm
Products: sprouts

LEBANON COUNTY

Sanger Farm
Jane Sanger
P.O. Box 256
Jonestown, PA 17038
717-865-7466
Description: NOFA-NJ-certified-
organic farm, wholesale, direct to
restaurants
Products: vegetables

LEHIGH COUNTY

Frost Hollow Herb Farm
Richard Mandelbaum
403 Washburn Avenue
Washington, NJ 07882
908-689-4067
Farm is in Easton, PA
Description: NOFA-NJ-certified-
organic farm, wholesale, retail

Products: medicinal herbs, some
edible herbs such as garlic and
basil

MONTGOMERY COUNTY

All Natural Market
30–36 Lancaster Avenue
Ardmore, PA 19006
610-896-7717
Description: natural foods store
Open: M–F 9am–9pm,
Sat–Sun 10am–6pm

Fresh Fields
1210 Bethlehem Pike
North Wales, PA 19454
215-646-6300

339 East Lancaster Avenue
Wynnewood, PA
610-896-3737

Description: natural foods
supermarkets

Genuardi's Family Markets
2850 Audubon Village Drive
Audubon, PA 19403
610-666-0414

3200 Ridge Pike
Eagleville, PA 19403
610-539-0660

1844 Bethlehem Pike
Flourtown, PA 19031
215-836-4300

737 Huntington Pike
Huntington Valley, PA 19006
215-379-6900

150 East Beidler Road
King of Prussia, PA 19406
610-265-1870

1758 Allentown Road
Lansdale, PA 19446
215-368-2893

1925 Norristown Road
Maple Glen, PA 19002
215-643-4567

1930 West Main Street
Norristown, PA 19403
610-539-0800

1000 Sandy Hill Road
Norristown, PA 19401
610-279-6494

2955 Swede Road
Norristown, PA 19401
610-277-5165

525 Sumneytown Pike
North Wales, PA 19454
215-699-7722

1400 North Charlotte Street
Pottstown, PA 19464
610-326-1795

70 Buckwalter Road
Royersford, PA 19468
610-948-6004

Description: supermarkets

Harvest Time
8080 Old York Road
Elkins Park, PA 19027
215-635-1107
Description: natural foods store
Open: M–F 9am–9pm, Sat 10am–
6pm, Sun 12pm–5pm

Nature's Harvest
101 East Moreland Road
Willow Grove, PA 19090
215-659-7705
Description: natural foods store
Open: M 10am–8pm, T–Sat 10am–
9pm, Sun 11am–6pm

PHILADELPHIA COUNTY

Center Foods
1525 Locust Street
Philadelphia, PA 19102
215-732-9000
Description: natural foods store
founded in 1977 with an in-store
deli featuring dishes made almost
exclusively from organically
grown products
Open: M–F 8am–8pm, Sat 10am–
6pm, Sun 11:30am–5pm

Essene Natural Foods Supermarket
719 South 4th Street
Philadelphia, PA 19147
215-922-1146
Description: natural foods store
started in 1970, large selection of
local organically grown produce
in season, bakery, deli, vegetarian
and macrobiotic cooking classes
Open: M–Sun 9am–8pm

Harry's Natural Food Store
1805 Cottman Avenue
Philadelphia, PA 19111
215-742-3807
Description: natural foods store,
certification not required
Open: M, T, Th, Sat, Sun 10am–
6pm, W and F 10am–8pm

Weavers Way Co-Op
559 Carpenter Lane
Philadelphia, PA 19119
215-843-2350
Description: natural foods co-op, certification not required
Open: M–F 10am–8pm, Sat 9am – 6pm, Sun 10am–4pm

Whole Foods Market
2001 Pennsylvania Avenue
Philadelphia, PA 19130
215-557-0015
Open: M–Sun 8am–10pm

929 South Street
Philadelphia, PA 19147
Opening in 1998

Description: natural foods supermarkets

PIKE COUNTY

Milford Natural Foods Store
203 6th Street
Milford, PA 18337
717-296-5966
Description: natural foods store
Open: M–Sat 10am–5:30pm, Sun 11am–5pm

Noll's Farm
Jerry Noll
1417 Springbrook Road
Shohola, PA 18458
717-296-6899
Description: NOFA-NJ-certified-organic farm

SNYDER COUNTY

Walnut Acres Organic Farm
Walnut Acres Road
Penn's Creek, PA 17862
717-837-0601
Description: certified organic farm founded in 1946, retail natural foods store, retail catalog, wholesale business

SUSQUEHANNA COUNTY

Mother & Son Farm
Joe Nunes
RR #1, Box 97
Springville, PA 18844
717-942-6598
Description: NOFA-NJ-certified-organic farm
Products: vegetables

WHOLESALE BROKERS

Albert's Organics
P.O. Box 624
Bridgeport, NJ 08014
609-241-9090
Description: full-service distributor of organically grown fresh foods, supports East Coast growers in season

Amazing Foods
237-67 Frelinghuysen Avenue
Newark, NJ 07114
973-621-1717

Hudson Valley Federation of Food Coops
Six Noxon Road
Poughkeepsie, NY 12603
914-473-5400
Description: natural foods warehouse; wholesale to buying clubs, co-ops, retail, mail order, and supermarkets; retail warehouse outlet

Indian Rock Produce
530 California Road
Quakertown, PA 18951
215-536-9600
Description: wholesale produce distributor that carries some local organic produce

Krystal Wharf Organic Produce
RD 2, Box 2112
Mansfield, PA 16933
717-549-8194
Description: delivery, mail order, shipper, wholesale, distributor of certified organic produce

NBA Organic Food Co-Op
329 Otter Street
Bristol, PA 19007
215-781-6303
Description: distributor of local organic produce; see retail listing under Bucks County
Open: W–F 10am–6:30pm, Sat 10am–4:30pm

ORGANIC FARMS WITHOUT THIRD-PARTY CERTIFICATION

Alloway Herbs
142 Kerlin Road
Salem, NJ 08079
609-935-0331
Description: farm raising herbs, seasonal on-farm retail stand, wholesale
Open: M–Sun all day, mid-April to frost

The Farm
3 Gully Road
Freehold, NJ 07728
732-462-2134
Description: farm raising vegetables and flowers, seasonal on-farm retail stand
Open: M–Sun 7am–9pm, mid-May to November

Genesis Farm
41 Silver Lake Road
Blairstown, NJ 07825
908-362-6735
Description: biodynamic farm with CSA program that includes flowers, herbs, fruits, vegetables

The Herb Garden
580 Zion Road
Egg Harbor Twp., NJ 08234
609-927-7327
Description: farm raising herbs, chickens, turkeys, geese, sheep; wholesale only

Hidden Hill Farm
55 Logan Road
Randolph, NJ 07869
973-584-4894
Description: farm raising grapes and herbs; wholesale only

Oak Grove Plantation
266 Oak Grove Road
Pittstown, NJ 08867
908-782-9618
Description: farm raising produce, Greenmarket at Union Square only

Parsonage Farm
135 Little York–Mt. Pleasant Rd.
Mt. Pleasant, NJ 08848
908-996-2350
Description: farm raising herbs, flowers, and vegetables; seasonal on-farm retail stand
Open: M–Sun all day, June to October

River Side Homestead Farm
3 Taylors Lane
Cinnaminson, NJ 08077
609-829-4992
Description: farm raising produce and straw; seasonal on-farm retail
Open: M–Sat 9am–6pm, June to October

Index by Restaurant